The Student's Pocket Guide to Personal Finance

Daniel K. Hartness

Introduction

First and foremost, Glory to God, without whom, not only could I not have written this book, but I would be utterly broken. Whether one student benefits from the words in this guide, or hundreds, the glory is to God alone and is worth every frustrated tear.

To my beautiful fiancé, Rachel, whom I've grown to love deeply through five years, a woman who is exemplary in all regards and whom I love beyond all reason and beyond all measure. Here's to our life together.

Stops on the Journey

Introduction

Money is something we all wonder about when we're young. Our relationship with it is often shaped by seeing our parents and others spending it or receiving it as gifts, particularly when we're much younger and active patrons of the Tooth Fairy. Our parents and family set the tone for what we think is the best, or at least 'normal' practice for money management. We grow up with increasing questions about how money works and for that matter, most aspects of personal finance. In our teens, we start hearing about taxes (especially when we start working), credit cards, investments, etc. But, it's hard getting answers even to the simple question of, "What is that?"

Frustrated, we gradually realize that money and finances, like religion, sex, and politics, are more of those topics people, especially adults, are uncomfortable talking about. As a result, most of us decide not to worry about those things any longer, or at least until we're an "adult." As we get older though and start having to 'adult' by working and paying bills, we realize just how much these topics matter. We wish, desperately, that someone had taught us about so many things related to money.

I was one of those students as were most of my friends and classmates. Money was culturally something we didn't discuss, especially with family, not until you're on the verge of going broke. Everyone would wait until the very last minute to reach out to their family for help. I can barely remember it being brought up in my house except as something my parents argued over.

I never understood why that was, why money was only ever brought up when people were angry. As I grew up, I saw firsthand many of the problems money causes, mainly among my friends and family. I witnessed multiple divorces, bankruptcies, losses of inheritances, and the smothering presence of increasing debt, all of these things stemming from mishandling finances and refusing to discuss them. Whenever I received money, I stuffed it in my pink piggy bank, I only associated it with yelling and anger, so I didn't want to mess with it. In a weird way, this was how I learned to save my money because hiding it was like second nature to me for my whole childhood.

My questions also increased as I entered high school and throughout college. I wanted to know why the government took taxes from my paychecks, what a credit card was and how to use it, how you're supposed to pay for college, and what people meant by the word 'investments'. I had an increasing interest in everything related to money and latched on to any piece of information I could find.

It was extremely hard to find any real answers though. When I asked people about any of these things, I was either told things that contradicted each other, or people would be vague and reluctant in their response. This left me with only one option: to figure it out on my own. This sucked. Every step in my financial journey felt overwhelming because I was faced with life challenge after life challenge without any real guidance. Don't get me wrong. I did have my immediate family supporting me in my choices and some friends to discuss

Introduction

ideas with, but encouragement from friends is not the same as life lessons and advice from someone with firsthand knowledge and experience. I ultimately had to learn how to manage my personal finances on my own, making plenty of mistakes along the way.

Why I've Written This Book

As I write to you now, I'm 24 years old and a recent graduate from Western Carolina University (WCU). Over the past 10 years, from high school through college, there was never a day that I didn't wish for someone to explain or warn me about some of life's most foundational and important principles in managing my personal finances. If you're remotely active on social media, you know I'm not the only young person who thinks that way. When we realize finances are much more complicated than we thought, we say, "Why didn't somebody warn us about this?!" or better yet, "Why weren't we taught this in school?"

The truth is, most of us aren't taught or are prepared for life's financial challenges, nor are we told the extra things we should be doing to prepare our financial futures. Because of this, we decide to "worry about it later" while we're young, and mourn over our ignorance when we're older.

During my six years of college (yeah that's right, I was a super-duper senior when I graduated), I talked with hundreds of students about finances. It was something that would come up naturally, and the other students enjoyed talking with someone who's actually willing to talk about it. Every conversation was long and intriguing, each ending with the student saying the same thing, "I wish someone told me about this stuff sooner." The students didn't say this because they were old, but because they realized they could have made different decisions when they were younger. They just wished they had a guide.

This is the place where most financial books fail. They often try to charm the readers into doing the thing that's best for them or saying that if they do a few simple things, everything's going to be wonderful. You can't charm people into being financially wise, simply by inspiring them to tell them what to do. No. You have to give people the tools by which to do all the things we'd view as wise. The tools being the guides, steps, and experienced knowledge that actually SHOWS them why such things are important and how to do each of them.

That's exactly why I've written this book. I want you and every student to know the important foundational pieces of personal finance. I want you to know them so that when you're my age, you won't have to wish someone helped you or told you how to prepare for your future. You'll be more prepared and confident than my generation with this book as YOUR Pocket Guide, the guide that tells you everything I've learned and gives you all the tools in a step-by-step manner, answering all the foundational questions we have as young students or the questions we didn't even know to ask. I wrote this book so you can learn all the things I had to find out the hard way through mistakes, without having to go through those same mistakes.

Here's a fair warning: with money comes topics like taxes and college debt. Personal finances aren't always going to be fun or sexy and are oftentimes the most boring when you're doing everything right, but I'm going to tell it all to you in a simple way. We're going to have a conversation, just you and me, student to student, and only get fancy when we need to.

Who Is This Book for?

I wrote this for you, the student, from high school all the way through college. It's easiest to learn the basics about personal finance when we're young before we've had the chance to rack up tons of debt without knowing where it came from. By learning the basics now, you'll be at more of an advantage than I and many others ever have been and start the best financial practices all the way from saving (Chapter 1) to investing (Chapters 10 & 11). My goal was to spare no expense and examine all of the things you may be curious about, worried about, or don't even know you need to be thinking about

Introduction

as students. We'll start off slow with why and how to save money (Chapter 1) and how to make money by working in high school (Chapter 2). We'll discuss how taxes work (Chapter 4) and how to master using a credit card (Chapter 5). After that, we'll deal with the huge decision of going to college and how to pay for it if you decide to go (Chapters 6 & 7-8), fully explain loans (Chapter 9), and end by talking all about investments and why they matter (Chapters 10 & 11). I'll answer your questions about these and give you tips and tricks I learned about them in my recent life, giving you the best head start possible. Ultimately, you'll learn about the most important factor of personal finance: being a good steward of your money so you and your family can live in a future that's financially secure and so you can truly help others.

I've written the chapters chronologically with each chapter building on the last. For example, I think you need a good grasp on saving money and why it's important in Chapter 1 before we can have a meaningful discussion about investing in Chapters 10 and 11. That's also why I've divided education into high school and college sections. Please feel free when reading though to continue through and don't feel like you're restricted just because of your grade. Whether you're a freshman in high school and want to get the best head start you can or a junior in college and want to learn all there is to know about personal finance, this book is the ideal pocket guide for you, one that you can always refer back to.

Thank you for joining me through this guide and I pray it will be a blessing to you, saving you a tremendous amount of time and heartache of learning things the hard way. So, what do you say? Think it's time we start talking money?

Section One: High School

Chapter 1: Where Are You Now and Where Do You Start?

So, you're in high school now, the place many students look forward to as a land of freedom and being treated more like an adult. I think high school is exactly that for most students. As we ascend the ranks of high school from "Fearful Freshman" to "Starry-Eyed Seniors," we experience more and more freedom. This starts in small ways of picking your classes and having more options for what you can eat for lunch. I was particularly glad I could have different sodas, teas, and Sobes instead of just milk cartons, even though cartoned chocolate milk was freaking delicious, especially after P.E. We also get more serious **freedoms**, like the ability to drive on our own and the chance to chill with our friends after school, away from home, making sure to obey your curfew of course.

With all of these new freedoms, you also have more **responsibilities**. Some of these definitely vary between students and your families, i.e your chore load, but most can relate to having to take good care of their vehicle and/or your increased homework load. Another even more important responsibility we have to manage is our money. It's a responsibility because, with our increased freedom, we can now get our first real jobs to earn money and have more control of what we spend it on. Our responsibility at this point is to manage the little stream of money we have, to make sure it's not wasted, and make sure it continues to flow. As we work, earn more money, and grow up, ideally that steady stream widens into a river with a strong current, directing that money to the best pools for you. There are many topics to touch on, and we'll take a closer look at them in the later chapters.

For now, let's continue to think about your current financial situation. On one hand is **freedom**- life is looking pretty sweet. You're living at home with tons of free time, your main worry being about finishing your homework quickly enough so you can do what you want with it. On the other hand is the **responsibility**- that freedom is going to cost you money.

New Costs

The first thing to look at is your car, your vehicle. This is the main way you're going to be traveling around, hanging out with friends in whatever capacity. Your car takes gas, and it adds up easily throughout the week, making it pricey to be a busy student. This can reasonably be $20-$30 each week, regardless of anything else you do, just by driving to school. That's going to be your typical expense, one that can vary a few dollars depending on the student and distance driven, but one you always depend on having. If you want to do extra things like dinner with friends occasionally or go watch the 50th new Marvel movie, that'll take extra cash too.

Finally, there's what I call the "easy" expenses, items that are really "low-cost" that are easy to justify. An example of this would be buying a daily soda, a Monster drink, or some sweet Starbucks goodness. We look at these as insignificant little things and say, "Ah, what the heck, it's only a couple of

7

dollars." It's very true that they're cheap, but those are the easiest and the sneakiest expenses that take cash quickly. Your $20 or $30 can be gone before you know it, and you already have a craving for your next drink. As young students, we can realize this fairly easily because our wallets are pretty thin anyway. Every $20 bucks we're handed feels precious and important, and if we hoard a few hundred we feel rich! Regardless of that being the common vibe among us, we are still quick to spend it because we don't really have bills.

Why Does Saving Money Matter?

This is where one of our new core financial responsibilities is found: properly saving our money. Don't worry! This doesn't mean that you should keep all of your money locked up in the bank or under your mattress. You can definitely buy things; you just need to make sure that all of your money is not being spent. Only spend a portion of your money, then take a portion of it and tuck it away. Save it. I'm sure you've run across plenty of people already who've told you it's good to save money. I know I sure have met plenty. It seems like EVERYONE knows saving is important, but rarely do they actually explain WHY it matters. This is where we often go wrong, shrugging off the idea of saving money. The majority of people don't truly understand the depths of why it matters.

It's actually advice that's been around for thousands of years and can even be found in the Bible. One such verse in Proverbs 21:20, our starting place, says "The Wise store up choice food and olive oil, but fools gulp their down" (NIV). The English Standard Version (ESV) translates it this way, "Precious treasure and oil are in a wise man's dwelling, but a foolish man devours it." It's a small verse, but one with heavy wisdom. Of course, if we ate all our food instead of storing some, we wouldn't have anything to eat later, especially when we're starving. The same goes for our money. It's wise to store it, to save it, rather than spending it all at once, or "gulping" it all down. That way, you'll have it when you need it.

The Student's Pocket Guide to Personal Finance

When you need it boils down to the certainty and uncertainty of the future. We're not only saving so we can freely do what we want later, but more importantly, so we have plenty of money when we, our family, and friends really need it. It takes us looking at and thinking towards the future, a future when we'll be older and wanting to retire. Gradually saving is the start of ensuring you'll be able to retire and live comfortably and safely. We know we are going to get older, so the earlier we start saving, the more we can prepare for when we are old.

This is hard, trust me, just like it sounds. Practicing restraint is by no means the normal thing, especially among others your age. It's hard to not "spend it if we got it," and you can't deny the fun of spending it. That's because we mainly focus on the current moment we're living in. Think back to the daily drink example I brought up at the beginning of the chapter. $2 or $3 for a drink truly doesn't sound like much, but that's because we're only thinking about our wants in the moment. We're not thinking about how much it costs over the whole week, let alone the whole year. A year of just buying your daily "cheap drink" at those prices would be $730 - $1,095. That's equivalent to a car payment or even a year of insurance. Crazy when you view it over the course of a year huh? Thinking about how quickly those costs add up makes every cent you have feel even more precious.

This brings me to the most important thing I've learned about saving money as a student: we're not good at predicting just how much money we're going to need, even for the next week. This is something you'll have to deal with much more quickly than you think, especially now that you're driving.

I was ecstatic to have a truck, a cherry-red '03 Ford Ranger, a joint gift from Dad and my MePaw (another southern word for Gramps). I loved it and always tried to take care of it and keep that bright red shine. Everything about it said, "Daniel." But I quickly underestimated what goes into keeping a vehicle going. I understood having to pay for gas, but I had no thoughts about changing the

9

Where Are You Now and Where Do You Start?

oil, rotating and replacing tires, cleaning the interior, or repairing any problems. The fun ran out quickly after driving around and going out to dinner for a few months. I loved doing those things with my friends, driving myself to school, and feeling like an adult making adult decisions, but the feeling of my wallet emptying every week was even more powerful.

I started realizing a basic principle about myself because of this, one that I think is true for almost everyone: I/we really didn't like spending money if I/we didn't have to. I knew that I could if I wanted to, that it was very fun to do extra things most days of the week, but felt even worse to get to the end of the week and noticed that I had nothing to show for it. Strangely, I decided to save a portion of any money I received. Just a few months into doing this, it helped me understand what it's like to have more stability and more confidence when I do need to spend some. From working a bit, saving money when I didn't need it and having my piggy-bank savings from childhood birthdays and Christmases, I had a good bit saved up over the next few months. By adopting this behavior, I was ready for those weird expenses I couldn't see coming.

They came quickly too. It wasn't long before I realized my truck was essentially a lemon. Every five to six months it seemed to have a new problem, most of them coming from the previous owner not taking care of it. First came an oil leak, then an antifreeze leak. Finally, when those were repaired and I thought I could breathe, my transmission went completely bad and had to be replaced. Yet another wonderful example of the previous owner being rough on the truck, never changing the oil, and I get stuck with the result.

It's easy to imagine even worse scenarios, right? Maybe you get in a wreck and your insurance isn't there to bail you out, or God forbid you have some serious health problems. It may not even be you, but it could be your family that hits a real rough patch and needs you more than ever. I get it, though, "Daniel, come on, I'm young! I don't need to worry about any of that!" It's true--you ARE young, but so am I. I was young when I got my first speeding ticket for $300+. I was young when I needed to scrape together $1,000 for an emergency fix on my truck. I was young when one of my oldest friends desperately needed something, anything to help sustain her and her family as both her and her husband lost their jobs. And I was really young, too young, when my dad had a heart attack.

What's the point? It's not that these same things are going to happen to you. You may go for a long time in life before a true emergency happens that demands past financial wisdom from you. But the ultimate point is that bad things, terrible things will happen, at some point. They always eventually do and the worst part about them is that we don't know when or how bad. There's always uncertainty. That's why you save money, so whenever they do happen, you're prepared and can face them head-on without the fear and worry so many people go through each day. You won't be living in fear of those possibilities. You'll be ready.

 **Saving:** *We save money not because we need it now but because we will most assuredly need it in the future. Despite the uncertainty of the future, we can be certain of that.*

Yeet Score

Saving is a concept we'll expound upon in every chapter. It's the crux of every discussion we're going to have, so we can't just abandon it to a small section, can we? I've got to give you the tools, not just charm. Those tools start here, by measuring your **Yeet Score**. Your Yeet Score shows the percentage of your money that is 'yeeting' out of your wallet and your bank account. Your money yeets out when you're spending it on things you don't need without you thinking much about it. And it can yeet out before you know it. As you can surely tell by now, making sure that all your money doesn't yeet away is

Where Are You Now and Where Do You Start?

serious business and that's EXACTLY why I'm calling this concept your Yeet Score. We need to be serious and scientific about it, so no laughing.

You want to keep your Yeet Score low, around 20-30%. Imagine, if you have $100, you don't want more than $20-$30 of it to be yeeted away. You'll feel some resistance to this as you start keeping track, but you'll start feeling the satisfaction of having your money saved up. You may not be the type of person who goes to Starbucks constantly or a religious soda drinker, but most of us have something that we're willing to spend more money on than we should. What do you buy often that you don't really need? I liked to buy video games every other week, several of my friends spent everything they had on getting more fishing equipment, and many students were all about having every bell and whistle they could on their vehicle, all being easy ways to yeet your money away.

That being said, start thinking about what you spend your money on in a typical week and the total amount you have each week. If you have a job or a type of allowance, this will make it easier to determine your Yeet Score. Add up the total you spent in the past week on things you don't need, divide it by the amount you typically start each week with, then you'll have your Yeet Score. Was it surprisingly high? Remember, we want to keep it knocked down to no more than 20-30%. It's a lot easier than we think to spend a lot of money, especially when we compare our extra expenses to the things we NEED to buy.

Now that you have your initial Yeet Score, even if it's in the safe range, we have a goal to work towards: to keep it there. Start keeping track of where your money goes each week, and you'll be in a better spot to think about saving. We'll dive more into the particulars of making money, budgeting, saving, and spending in the next two chapters, but first, I'll tell you about the best way I've found to keep track of your money.

EveryDollar

We live in a time where there's some awesome tools at our disposal. They make most aspects of your personal finances significantly easier to manage, especially tracking your money. One I recommend for you is an app called EveryDollar, created by Dave Ramsey. Dave has a long history of helping many Americans work their way out of debt and warning them against its severe negative effects. He helps turn their life around and get them back on track starting with the foundations of saving just like we are. One of the big ways he helps them is by encouraging them to properly budget. I explain budgeting to folks as knowing where every one of your dollars goes, how, and why. You should always be aware of how much money you have, so you're never caught off guard by surprise expenses; you're in complete control of your budget. This is where EveryDollar is excellent.

You plug in every typical expense you have on weekly or monthly bases and the amount of money you have to spend total. There are categories for just about every normal expense you can think of, and you have the ability to add extra ones if your situation is somewhat unique. Once you've listed them all, you are then given the total amount of money you have leftover. This amount is your free or 'extra' money, money you don't necessarily have a plan for and it doesn't HAVE to go towards anything. It can be your fun money. In chapter 3, we'll talk about using the app to closely budget your paycheck and what to do with your free money. For now, download the app and start getting used to it. You can constantly make updates to it as your financial situation changes either with switching jobs or taking on more bills.

The other helpful feature of EveryDollar is that you can continually log each of your payments as you make them. By no means are you expected to be a master of your money at this point, but this is how you can start down that path. EveryDollar acts as a mini spreadsheet you can keep in your pocket. Start getting in the habit of logging everything you spend money on, even if it's

13

something as insignificant as a drink or a snack. In part, this will be another way of knowing exactly how much money you have at any point, but developing this habit of pausing after every purchase/expense lets you think about why you just spent that money. You're giving your money more meaning, realizing how quick and easy it is to spend, while also thinking about what it took to acquire it. As you start working and having different expenses, this habit will make it much easier to make decisions with your money. It will help you determine how much you need to save, and ensure you don't overspend.

Summary

To start our personal financial journey, we have to begin with the basics of budgeting and saving. Mastering these habits now in high school will pave the way for the other chapters and for the rest of your life. The key to a successful journey is good tools to help you along the way. Thankfully, we live in a time where tools like EveryDollar are available at our fingertips!

Tools for the Journey

- ***The Wealthy Barber by David Chilton:*** *The very first financial book I ever read. Not only did this book teach me the importance of saving, but it gave me a completely different outlook on money. Chilton does an excellent job of breaking things down so anyone can understand it. I highly recommend it!*

- ***EveryDollar:*** *The best financial phone app I can recommend. It's easy to use and keeps your finances very well organized. This will be one of your best tools as you continue through this pocket guide. For every new bill you have and every new dollar you make, EveryDollar will be ready for it.*

- ***Dave Ramsey Show and Marko - Whiteboard Finance:*** *Check these guys out on YouTube. Not only is it important to read and practice good financial habits, it's important to listen to the advice of more experts. Dave and Marko are two of the best I can recommend. Dave has helped thousands of people solve their financial difficulties and adopt wise habits. Marko always has good current tips and tricks for a variety of situations.*

Chapter 2: How Do I Get a Job?

We briefly touched on the newfound freedom and responsibilities faced when going through high school and how becoming more conscious of our personal finances should be an important part of that. Before you can really start saving money, though, we need to talk about increasing the money we have. There are two ways to do this: increase your income or reduce your expenses. I call this the **maximization rule,** and it's one of the most basic rules of personal finance. They act as a strong exercise that you can think through whenever evaluating your financial situation.

When thinking about the typical high school student, we can apply these rules pretty quickly. The easiest thing you can do, like we talked about in the last chapter, is to reduce your expenses, mainly only spending your money when it's absolutely necessary, like on gas, for example. You can limit the amount you go out to eat for example, decreasing the amount of money you spend on "fun." Now, this sounds more boring than it has to be. You can still do things with your friends, just choose activities that are cheaper or even free. You could go for a hike or walk at your local park instead of going to the movies or combine your money to buy a large pizza rather than individual meals. There are a lot of options here to reduce the money you spend while still having fun. As a student, you can reduce your expenses only so much. If you reduce them too much, you'll eventually stop paying for things you need. This would boil down to bills, food, gas, car repairs, etc. depending on the person. Once you've reduced most of your extra expenses, that leaves increasing your income as your next objective. You can increase your income the most by getting a job, and most students get their first while in high school.

Why Get a Job in High School?

This is a question I've been asked by many high school and college students. You may be wondering the same thing because, at least for the majority of students, you don't have massive bills like rent while you're in high school. Working isn't purely about paying for your bills, though. That's definitely a part of it, but there are longer term goals that matter even more. Learning to save, managing a budget, and developing a work ethic are just some of those. Getting a job in high school helps you become more responsible with your money. You care about every cent you earn for exactly that reason- you've earned it. And that's exactly what money is, what you're given in exchange for your time/work. That's why you begin to value it. You dedicated hours that could have been used for more entertaining things.

Furthermore, a job shows you what it's like to work for someone else. It's a situation where you have to learn to be more respectful of your bosses or clients, do a good job, and how to follow directions. These are skills you'll carry with you for the rest of your life into whatever career or field you go into. Patience goes along with this, too. It's likely that your first job will involve hard work and a lot of manual labor. Don't be dismayed by that. It'll make every dollar you earn that much sweeter and will really help develop your work ethic.

Your **work ethic** is what your bosses are going to care about the most. Can they rely on you to do your job without having to constantly be told what to do? Are you someone they can trust? Do you try your best to come in with a positive attitude? Do you come in on time? These are all traits employers will consider when hiring you, and it all starts with your first job. This is the time when you can make honest mistakes without too much worry, but more importantly, it gives you time to perfect being a responsible worker. Doing this helps you gain positive work experience that you can put on your resume when applying for better jobs, those that pay more and are more interesting to you. Your bosses will be glad to give you good references and recommend you for other positions. Having a strong work history like this will help you get more jobs as you get older. Employers will be more apt to hire you because you'll have more work experience.

Finally, it's nice to actually be earning your own money. You're freer this way, not having to depend on your parents. That's the biggest benefit in my opinion. You earn your own money and get to decide what you want to do with it. You're another step closer to adulthood, without having full adult responsibilities. It's a sweet time to be making money because most of what you make, you'll get to keep since you have few expenses. So, let's make all that we can!

How to Get a Job

This can be a scary thing, especially when you've never worked for someone before. But don't worry, there's a whole process we can go through to make this much easier. To start, we need to think about what options are available to you. You're in high school, so your time is usually limited to evenings and summers. We also have to consider what jobs are best for you based on who you know and where you live.

1. Identify Where to Start/What Work Is Interesting

To walk through this process, we have to consider the reasonable amount of time each evening you can work, probably only three-four hours during the school year. In addition, you have the weekends to work extra if you want. Since your main work hours are in the evening, that does have a few limitations on what you can do. With that in mind, your golden opportunities for more hours will be during the summer and over school breaks.

When we think about high school jobs, service jobs are the first thing that comes to mind: flipping burgers, slinging tacos, or stocking grocery shelves. These definitely aren't the most fun jobs, especially when your Cookout gets slammed for a dinner rush, but there are good reasons why these jobs are the most popular for students. Fast food chains and grocery stores are always hiring, making it almost an accomplishment if you can't get a job with one. Unless you've committed some serious crimes, they should be open to anyone with basic reading skills. As a whole, student workers are constantly in flux, starting and quitting these jobs at the drop of a hat, allowing you room to apply for nearly a guaranteed job. The downside to these can often be only making minimum wage, which is $7.25/hr as I'm writing, and they leave you exhausted. You'll be busting your butt. That means getting hot and sweaty, and likely having to do several hours of customer service work, too. These aren't the best jobs by any means, but they are likely the most numerous available. Most towns have fast-food chains, local restaurants, or a Walmart that need additional help. You may even find some that offer to pay upwards of $10-$11/hour. It will just depend on where you live. If you find one that pays more, smelling like the fast-food you're making might be worth it!

Waiting tables might be a more attractive choice for some of you. You are paid less initially as an hourly rate by your restaurant, but you have the potential to earn good money through tips. The upside of waiting tables is you won't be dealing with the craziness of a kitchen or killing your back shuffling

How Do I Get a Job?

jugs of milk into Walmart's fridges, but 95% of your job will be customer service. Jobs like this will likely be more appealing to you if you're extroverted, meaning you really like being around and talking to lots of people. If you're mainly introverted, this could be an exhausting line of work. In fact, your tips depend on good customer service, which requires a good deal of social energy. This is a really good skill to learn, and you'll find that the jobs I recommend the most give the chance to learn these skills well. With waiting tables, you're rewarded mostly based on how good of an experience you make for each of your diners: making sure their drinks are topped off, smiling, asking if they need anything, and making light conversation really make a difference. Remember, though, this type of job isn't for everyone. Dealing with lots of people can be unbelievably frustrating, especially those that are very demanding, even while you're trying your best. It's good to consider jobs like this because of the money, but there's less customer-intensive jobs if that's more your speed: lifeguarding, working concessions (like at a movie theater), being a cashier, and bagging groceries. With these alternatives, you still get to build your customer-relation skills and have a guaranteed wage, but you can avoid the overwhelming pressure of working fast food.

 **Customer Service:** *I mentioned customer service is important because it's one of the best ways you can learn to communicate with different types of people at a young age. Every customer is completely different, something you'll notice quickly. Learning to talk to customers is a skill that'll translate into many facets of your life, all involving dealing with people and being under pressure. You'll be more comfortable in interviews, going to places where you have to meet new people, and even managing stressful situations.*

Working for Myself

Maybe you don't want to work for a company or you live far from town. I grew up in the small, rural town of Murphy, North Carolina, and lived a good 15-30 minutes from town, depending on who I was driving behind and if I was coming from my mom or dad's house. It was one of those towns where people ACTUALLY walked uphill both ways to get to school. There also weren't too many job options for high schoolers apart from fast-food and local grocery stores, so several of us took a different approach: we started our own lawn care businesses. Those of us who did had small two-door trucks, and our parents helped us purchase a small push mower and a weed-trimmer (called weed-eater by us more country folk) to get started and occasionally helped us with gas. Other students in our class started their own baby-sitting businesses. The babysitters didn't have much in the way of costs like us mowers, apart from gas.

What did both of these types of jobs have in common? Their flexibility. We worked for ourselves. It was up to each of us to get our own clients, to negotiate how much we charged, and to schedule our jobs. Even though mowing and babysitting are drastically different types of work, they're similar in those business styles. Maybe it's appealing to you, too. You have the freedom of scheduling your own jobs, essentially whatever works best for you and the client.

Sometimes with lawn care, you can have a whole week to get a job done, meaning your timing is much more flexible, just as long as you finish the job. With multiple clients, you'll experience a range of difficulties with your jobs. For example, I had one excellent client named Chuck, who paid me $25 for mowing his lawn, no matter how long it took or how much his grass grew, and I would mow it every week. He'd also always pour me a cold glass of apple juice whenever I finished, one of the best treats you could ask for when you get hot and sweaty.

How Do I Get a Job?

You can see the benefit to this type of job. Some days I'd finish in 30 minutes, and other times it could take over an hour. These are the most ideal clients. I had others who fought with me over every dollar, and refused to pay me more than $10/hr, despite using my own equipment. It's the same when babysitting. You could babysit a good kid who's calm and obedient, or it could be a kid with limitless energy who acts like they run purely off Mountain Dew and memes. The jobs need to be chosen with care. Sometimes, it's better to "fire" a client you butt heads with or refuse a job that you know you'll hate than it is to be miserable.

Pricing the Job: *Here's one of the best lessons I've learned through my lawn care business. When talking to potential clients, parents/lawn-owners, negotiate your prices by the job rather than settling for an hourly rate. This basic principle allows you to make more money and learn A TON about talking business. Let's walk back through the previous examples. It's important to remember, no two jobs are the same. Maybe you come across an easy lawn care job. You need to trim a few hedges, mow a yard that would take 10-20 minutes, and pull a few weeds. Comparatively, maybe you only need to babysit a well-behaved child for two hours while the parents want to go on a late dinner date and the kid's in bed. In either case, there's not much to those jobs. You can say, "Yeah, I'll do it for $20-$30 and have it done in no time"(or whatever you deem reasonable based on your situation).The point is that even though those jobs are pretty quick and easy, you want to make sure you're paid a fair share. With lawn care, it's not worth sticking to the $10/hr standard. On smaller jobs, you wouldn't make anything, and on tough jobs, it may eat too much into your fuel costs. Learning to negotiate will come in handy when you're interviewing for your career or asking for raises.*

Delivery

This is the last job type I'll dive into. I just want to get your wheels turning about possible jobs that are out there and what interests you the most.

The Student's Pocket Guide to Personal Finance

Delivery jobs have become incredibly popular, especially with students. These are jobs where you use your vehicle and deliver something to customers. There's the standard pizza delivery. Then there are the most recent additions from more 'freeform' delivery companies like DoorDash, GrubHub, and PostMates. You take food from a 'partner' restaurant, or even groceries from a market, and then deliver it to the customer. Let's look at both of these types and why delivery can be an awesome choice.

If you're a standard pizza delivery deliverer, you'll be paid an hourly wage as well as tips. Similar to waiting tables, the wage is too small on its own, and the majority of your pay will come from customer tips. Like any tip-based job, your potential for earning money is higher than a standard job, but it also means you can have some rough shifts where you don't make much. It depends on both the customer and how well you serve them.

Pizza delivery is likely the most relevant standard delivery job to you because almost every town has at least one pizza place. Eating pizza is almost as American as every town having a Waffle House. We wouldn't be the USA without them. Pizza companies pay slightly above minimum wage, and some will increase your pay if you take specialized training on baking pizzas. That's definitely not bad to start. When you weigh in the additional tips you'll be making, it starts to sound really good! Of course, you'll spend most of your time on the road, not speeding at all, trying to make those deliveries as fast as you can. The more deliveries you make, the more tips you take. Speeding won't make much of a difference. Shaving a minute or two off your route isn't going to rake in a fortune and going 5mph extra won't skyrocket your hourly deliveries. Most of your time will be spent either waiting on the food or waiting on the customer.

Your pizzeria will have a maximum distance for their route they'll set you on, meaning they'll almost never take a delivery that's too far from the store, the most being 15-20 minutes away. So time's not going to be your biggest issue. The customers will. Taking your time, and being polite and mannerly is going to be a much bigger deal than being in a hurry to get to the next delivery. Being friendly and smiling at the customer can be the difference between even getting tipped and getting stiffed. It's true for any tipped delivery service. Although, as my friends and I who DoorDashed and delivered pizzas can tell you, being friendly to the customer doesn't guarantee a tip, it definitely increases the chances of getting one.

You need to know that tipping is primarily cultural, meaning we all have slightly different views on tipping. Some folks view tipping as highly important, while others think it's just included in the service. That being said, you're going to get stiffed when doing this type of work. It won't be often, but you'll run into a customer every now and then that takes your food with no tip. The first time I was stiffed, I brought $150 worth of BoJangles to a lady around 9pm. This was a huge order, consisting of about four whole chickens and two gallons of sweet tea, and of course no tip. I was pissed! It only lasted a few minutes, because my next order tipped $6, but it still makes for a good story! More often, you'll have nice customers, but you'll have a few you can complain to your friends about.

The other companies I mentioned, Doordash, Grubhub, and Postmates, are similar to pizza delivery but allow you to have even more independence. You get to work for yourself, working whenever you want. I worked with Doordash a lot as a college student, and it quickly became my favorite of these types, what I'm calling "freeform delivery" companies.

Here's how it works:

Doordash

First, download the Dasher app and make an account with them. You'll use it for everything. Once you've registered as an official Dasher, you'll have a couple of options. You'll notice that the home screen of the app is a Google Map view of your surrounding area. You'll know where you can start dashing because there will be red-lined areas, called dash zones. These are typically fairly wide areas where there's plenty of restaurants. This means that folks can use the Doordash delivery app or website to order food from them, then have someone like you deliver it. The dash zone will be various shades of red depending on the number of customers ordering DoorDash deliveries. It will start at a faint pink, indicating there's little activity, to a very bright red for 'Very Busy'. That's the best time to go. Pick the area you want to dash in, and you can either schedule your own time or just drive to the outlined dash zone and begin a dash. This is where you get to see one of the great things about DoorDash, which is that you can schedule your own hours. You're not at the mercy of a manager. Use that scheduling to your advantage.

Start your dash and then find an area to park your car that's near a majority of the local restaurants. The parking lot of a fast food chain or a grocery store works best. You won't know 100% of all the restaurants that are dashable, but being near them constantly is key. This will be your **hub**. After every delivery, come back to this spot. This will give you quick access to the majority of restaurants and, more importantly, will increase your chances of getting assigned orders first. DoorDash's algorithm assigns deliveries to the dasher closest to the requested restaurant.

 **Dasher Hub -** *You want to pick a spot that's in the heart of town, where a good number of restaurants are located. This will make you more likely to be assigned deliveries near you, and you'll have less to drive. You'll see a few flame icons in your dash zone, called hot spots, that show you the areas where the most orders are often placed. You can use those to figure out a good hub to come back to wait on orders.*

Let's talk about the deliveries themselves and what to expect. The norm will be as simple as walking into the restaurant or going through a drive through, and telling either the hostess/cashier you're here to pick up a DoorDash order for the name assigned to the order. Your Dasher app will have the full information for each delivery. The name of the customer (which you'll need to give to the restaurant), every item on the order, and the delivery address. For each step in the delivery (arriving at the restaurant, picking up the food, then delivery), the app has you verify you've completed each one. Having this makes you check for each item on the order before you leave. Take it from me, one of the most successful ways to lose a tip is to arrive 20 minutes ahead of time to the customer's house, then realize they had two drinks you didn't get. After you've checked off each item, The Dasher app will then give you the option to GPS track the delivery address and will tell you the estimated time to reach it by. From my experience, you'll always be given plenty of time, allowing for absurd traffic, slow service at the restaurant, or getting totally lost. When you get close to your destination, check to see if there are any special delivery instructions. Do they want you to knock, hand it directly to them, is there a gate code, apartment number, etc. After you drop it off, then let the customer know you've made the delivery through the app verification. Then you get paid!

Payment

There's a minimum amount you're guaranteed to make with every delivery, called your delivery fee. This is typically around $3 as experienced from my group of dashers. A customer then has the option of adding a tip. Often, they'll determine their tip ahead of the delivery, and you'll be able to see it before accepting the order. You can also see the address beforehand. This is convenient l because you can choose which orders are really worth it to you. It's also nice if you recognize the address and know they're a bad customer. Don't get too trigger happy, though. Every Dasher has an acceptance rate score. If it drops too low, you'll be given fewer and fewer orders, so only refuse the worst ones you come across. I mainly refused those that I knew would be too far to drive for the small tip or if it was an address I recognized that habitually didn't tip.

As you get used to dashing, you'll start to notice the busiest times are often lunch rushes from 11am-2pm, and after folks get home work from 6pm-9pm. Try to plan your dashes around those times and the days that are often the busiest like the weekend. In addition, Doordash will sometimes offer what's called "Peak Pay." These are time slots that they know are often busy for a zone, and if they don't have enough dashers scheduled to work, they offer additional cash per order to entice you to sign-up. And don't worry, it can be enormous. I've dashed on some weekends in busy downtown areas with $8.00 peak pay. That's right, an additional $8 per delivery on top of tips! Dashing during Peak Pay can triple or quadruple your profits per dash. Peak Pay times were so profitable, in fact, my friends and I sometimes only dashed during them and still grossed $20-$30/hr.

This is ultimately the reason I really recommend DoorDashing as your primary or even as a side job on the weekends or the evening. It can be very rewarding, and can be easily balanced with school, family, or an additional job if you just focus on the Peak Pay time slots.

See if any of the Freeform Delivery companies are available near you and see if it's a good fit. If not and you're still interested in delivery, local pizzerias or other restaurants are your strongest option.

2.   Identify Easy Ways In

Now that you've been thinking about the types of jobs that are around you, what you're interested in, and what works best with your schedule, you should also consider if there's any easy-to-get job opportunities available to you. In essence, does your family run a small business in the area or are there local business owners you know well and are family friends? Perhaps your parents know people in the community you could work for.

How Do I Get a Job?

Thinking about it a different way, if you want to try babysitting or lawn care, the easiest clients you can start with would be your friends, family, or neighbors. Start with whatever is the most low-hanging fruit for you. My example comes first from my friend Addison, who brought me into his small mowing business. I got to know and work for a few of his clients, then inherited them after Addison moved back to his home state of Florida. After that, my best opportunity came from a man named Tim Pratt. I met him during my sophomore year when I joined our high school shooting team. You know you're in the South when your high school has a shooting team. One of our disciplines was shooting clay pigeons, and Tim was our coach. We became fast friends, and he quickly became a strong mentor for me. Now, I always refer to him as my second dad. Tim was a log cabin builder in Murphy and owned a development where he'd built many cabins called Vineyard Creek Estates. There was a lot to take care of in the development, from a ton of grass to a large vineyard. Tim often offered to pay many of the shooting team kids to do yard maintenance like mowing, weed-eating, pruning trees, and doing other chores for some extra cash. So, start asking yourself, "What opportunities are available to me based on people I know?"

3. Applying for the Job

Now comes the fun part, actually applying. For your traditional job, you'll fill out an application with your information and turn it in to either the owner or manager of the business. This is becoming more of an online process, but some businesses may still hand you a physical form. Either way, it starts with you visiting their website, where the hiring process may be detailed, or walking into the business itself and asking them how you can apply. Family-owned, local businesses are more likely to have a physical form or another hiring process, while large widespread companies, like Domino's, Wal-Mart, etc., will have an easy online application process.

The Student's Pocket Guide to Personal Finance

Applying for the job won't necessarily land you the job, but it can get you an interview. If they're interested in your application, they'll call or email telling you to come in. This part can be pretty terrifying, much more so than asking for and turning in the form. Don't worry, though. We all have to go through this. When you sit down with the hiring manager, be respectful and let them welcome you, then ask you some questions. For a high schooler, don't expect it to be a very complex interview. It's a very standard procedure to hire students and start them working. The interviewer mainly wants to see if you're a respectful young adult who wants to work there and to see if you have some previous experience (and if not, if you're willing to learn). Interviewing at this stage in your life is, again, good experience for you. It's something you'll get more and more comfortable with.

On that note, apply to plenty of businesses, unless you know you have a sure thing through folks you know. While places like Wal-Mart or McDonald's aren't likely to turn you away, it's never a bad idea to have some back-up plans.

Going door to door for new business is also part of this third step. When I started my mowing business, I was really scared. I had very little experience talking to complete strangers and hated the idea of asking random people if I could work for them. I'd convince myself before every attempt that they'd tell me no, and would often use that as an excuse to not even try. My parents, specifically my dad, encouraged me through this, though, encouragement I want to give to you too.

He said, "Cub (my very masculine nickname, of course), it's honestly a scary world, not just when you're trying to work for people. Every day you have the chance of being told 'no' for something, something you probably really want. But, if you're too scared of being told 'no', then you're never going to put yourself in the position to be told, 'Yes!'"

How Do I Get a Job?

Those words gave me the kick in the butt to at least try. They helped me realize that the worst thing that can happen is that I can be told 'no', but at least I'll know for sure. If I never attempt to ask folks for their business, I'll never have the potential to get their business. Take the leap and go for it. When you get your first client, your first lawn, or your first baby to care for, especially on your own, you'll know it's possible to do this.

Summary

Getting and starting your first job can be challenging, overwhelming, and downright scary. But you can do it. Take your time, look around and break the process down into these three steps. This will help you learn what it's like to work for others, earn money, and appreciate that money because you worked for it. You can continue to get better jobs through your experience. And even more so, for the purposes of learning about finances, it gives you a way to make your money. You need income before we can start practicing the best methods of managing it.

Let's move into the next chapter and figure out what we should do with that money!

Tools for the Journey

- **Snagajob.com and Indeed.com:** *Two of the best websites to find job opportunities in your area. You can find who's hiring, what they're paying, and apply for jobs using these sites.*

- **GMail and Google Drive Suite:** *If you don't already have a Gmail account, create one. Not only will you need an email account to help you manage your accounts on your apps and other websites, but it will give you access to the free suite of tools like docs and sheets on your Google Drive. Instead of having to buy Microsoft Office, you can take advantage of Google's versions of these applications and keep them saved online.*

Chapter 3: Here's My Paycheck! But What Do I Do with It?

Now we get to talk money, the greenbacks, the cheddar, the dough, the cold-hard cash you're busting your butt for! Maybe you've gotten your first job and got your first paycheck. Maybe you've been working for a while and have gotten a few but are unsure what to do with it. Or, maybe you're reading on ahead. Either way, let's first explore using our money!

Create a Bank Account

The first thing to do is set up a bank account, specifically your checking and savings accounts. For some, this may be a bit obvious, but it's important we cover the basics.

Picking a bank may be something you're wondering about. At this stage in your life, you don't need to worry much about which one you choose. In fact, most teenagers will set up their accounts in the same banks as their parents.

This way, you can ask your parents specific questions about banking and, as a neat function, your parents can be co-managers of your accounts. The good thing about that is they can help you better manage your money and deposit some into your account if you need it. If the idea of sharing your bank account with your parents sounds horribly lame (I definitely thought so), then you can just open your own. The only thing you really need to keep in mind is to choose a bank that doesn't charge you a lot of fees to open or maintain accounts.

Fees vary from bank to bank, but you can be pretty safe from them if you stick with a local bank, meaning ones that aren't large brand names like Bank of America or BB&T. Local banks and credit unions have an easier to understand fee structure, with most of them not being hidden from you. Nevertheless, fees are typically very low. Credit unions in particular have little to no fees. The difference is that credit unions are not for profit, where standard banks are. This is why you'll notice much lower fees with credit unions. The catch with them is that some are membership based, meaning an annual fee to be a member. Others like my first bank, State Employees' Credit Union (SECU), require you to have a direct family relation to an employee of your state.

It's a very easy process and doesn't cost you anything. You simply walk into the bank of your choice and tell them you'd like to open both accounts. You'll sit down with a representative, give them your information, including your Social Security number, and then you'll need to deposit a minimum amount for each. For most bank accounts, you're required to keep a minimum amount of cash in each to keep the account open. For checking and savings, this is normally around $20. While you're there, you'll want to order a **debit card**. This card pays for items and services directly from your checking account, another reason why it's important to keep some money in it. Your bank account is going to be the key to everything related to your money. The bank will be the main way you move your money around and spend it when you need to. You'll use your bank to store and save your money so you don't have to keep up with much loose cash. With bank accounts, you're all set-up for your job.

Download Your Banking App: *Every bank has a mobile app that you can download. This is an enormously useful tool that you need. It allows you to check your account balances at anytime and anywhere. More importantly, you can use it to instantly transfer money between your accounts. This makes saving via the 10% rule easier. As soon as your money is deposited, log in with your phone app and pay yourself by transferring it into your savings. In emergencies, you can also move money from your savings account into your checking, giving you instant access when you need it.*

Money Market vs. Savings Account: *While your money rests in your bank accounts, you'll notice you're earning interest. Basically, while your money is in the bank, the bank borrows it from you and uses it to give loans to people. In turn, the bank pays you a small percentage of that money bank in the form of interest. Each type of account has a different interest rate, with checking accounts having the lowest. Your savings account has a higher rate, encouraging you to keep that money in the bank. Rather than keeping your nest egg and emergency funds in a standard savings account, I recommend you open a **money market account**. These are almost identical to savings accounts. The main differences are that it requires a higher minimum of cash to be kept in, typically more than $100. This is fine, as this is meant to be your nest egg anyway. The benefit to the money market account is you're paid a greater deal of interest than a savings account. That money may as well earn you more interest while you're building up your savings!*

Getting Paid

This varies from job to job. For babysitting, landscaping, or doing small jobs, you'll normally be handed cash or a hand-written check. If you've written a check, you can either deposit it at your bank into your checking account so you can move it around, or have the bank teller cash it. With most banking apps, you can also digitally deposit the check by taking pictures of it. For a normal hourly wage job, you'll either receive a check in the mail or be paid through a method called **direct deposit**. This is also how you'll be paid from the freeform delivery companies like Doordash and Grubhub. They deposit your earnings into your bank account, usually weekly.

Finally, if you're working as a waitress, delivery driver, where you receive tips, you'll receive some regular hourly pay, typically at the reduced rate I mentioned, and your tips will be separate. For a pizza company like Domino's, you keep all of the cash customers pay you until the end of your shift, usually in a type of lockbox. Your manager will then count the receipts and tell you how much you owe them. If you delivered $100 worth of food, that means you would owe Domino's at least $100. Then, the leftovers would be your tips. If you wait tables, there are two common ways you'll be paid your tips. First, some restaurants and cafes have a tip sharing system. The system depends on the type of restaurant, but it can range from every waiter paying a percentage of their tips to the bussers, folks who clean-up/bus the tables, and to the bartenders because they'll make the drinks for customers. All of the wait staff could share tips as well, meaning they split the total number of tips. The most common way is pocketing your tips. Customers either tip you on their card or leave cash on the table, and you keep it. In this case, you'll have to report the amount you make or some percentage of it to your business/restaurant so they can report it on your taxes.

What Do I Do with My Money?

Now you've gotten paid, and it feels good. Whatever you were paid, you earned it, and there's nothing like the feeling you get from your first paycheck. Here's where the important challenge comes in. Before you do anything with that money, stop for a minute and appreciate the fact you worked hard for it. At this age, every dollar you earn is precious.

Here's My Paycheck! But What Do I Do with It?

Now, reflect back to the first chapter when we talked about saving and spending. What are your typical costs per **pay period**? Compare that with the money you make per week. This shows you the beginning of your budget: the amount of the money you need to live on, then the money you have leftover. With this, you're ready to calculate other things to do with your money: saving, giving, eventually investing, and a few fun things.

Pay Period: *Every job pays you on a different schedule called a pay period. This can be every week, every two weeks, or once a month. That has to factor into your calculations.*

Saving Money

Like I said in Chapter 1, everyone knows that saving money is smart and that bad things happen in life. Despite everyone knowing this, it's rarely put into practice. Most of us would rather just spend the money and have as much fun as we can, regretting those decisions while cringing as our debit card is suddenly declined. While you're in high school with your expenses low, it's the ideal time to forge that habit of constantly saving. The easiest way to get in that habit is by saving a portion of each paycheck before doing anything else with that money. This means that before you even pay a bill with it, you put some in your savings account first. Before you pay anyone else, you're paying yourself. The ideal amount to start with is 10% of each check, or, whatever money you make.

I learned this concept from reading a great book called, *The Wealthy Barber* by David Chilton, which was given to me by Tim. When he realized that I was becoming increasingly interested in personal finances and was prepping for college, he gifted it to me. Chilton, introduces this 10% rule as the foundation of his book. Essentially, if you don't remember anything else after reading it, remember that rule. That was exactly my takeaway from it, and I applied it to every dollar I earned. I suggest that you make that your starting place, too. Once you start saving 10% of each piece of your income or each paycheck, it quickly becomes a habit. You'll do it without thinking.

This method guarantees you don't spend all of your money whenever you get it because it's the first thing you do. Your excitement will start to build when you see your savings account growing steadily. You're building up your money for when you need it while the majority of students around you are spending theirs, completely unprepared for the unexpected. This is essentially what I meant by the concept of paying yourself first.

Living on Less

As you grow up, go to college, start a career, move to a home, this savings concept helps you in another way. You learn to live on less.

You're paying yourself first with your 10%, right? This means that you'll have to use the remaining amount for everything else, and you instinctively start learning how to live only on that 90%. This works because you don't really 'need' all of the money in your check in the first place. We all have that desire to 'spend it if we got it' because it's much more fun that way. You won't even notice you're missing that money after a while. You'll be focused on working with the remaining budget. This makes it all the more satisfying when you notice your savings constantly growing while you're getting along just fine. In addition to this, you'll start discovering more and more ways to save money because you're much more aware of spending it, especially how much everything costs. This is really important later on when living by yourself and/or going to college.

Develop a Savings Goal

It's good to give yourself a savings goal to work towards. You have something to accomplish, and it's much more rewarding as you watch your money slowly reach your goal. I went about this by picking an amount of money that sounded like a huge number to me, like $1,000. I started working in

Here's My Paycheck! But What Do I Do with It?

lawn care my sophomore year, then eventually worked in a vineyard making about $10/hr throughout high school. I felt like I was making bank at that rate. I didn't need to spend much, so I decided that I would just save it, buying the occasional video game, of course. $1,000 sounded like loads of money, and I wanted to be able to see that I had $1,000 in my bank account. It felt like a reasonable goal for high school, one I wanted to achieve by the time I graduated. I figured some of that thousand would go a long way towards college, wherever I decided to go. After all, high schoolers hear all the time that college is expensive.

   The crazy thing about my goal was I hit it a little after my first summer of working had ended (heading into junior year). I couldn't believe it. "Is $1,000 really not that much?" After I started looking more into college prices, I realized $1,000 DEFINITELY isn't much. This is one of those times I'm thankful for my mom's nagging about researching college early as junior year. The more I worked, the more I had to up my goal, using thousand dollar increments. I eventually graduated high school with hitting my goal of $6k in the bank, a huge confidence boost going into college. I recommend you take your savings goals $1k at a time, too. Every thousand you save is a HUGE milestone, and you'll realize more and more how quickly you can reach it. For the average student, I recommend you aim for $5k as your savings goal for the end of the summer after you graduate. It's a good amount of money that can help you with college, an apartment, or a car. It will also take care of most emergencies you're likely or unlikely to have at your age. Some of you may blow past this goal easily. SWEET! If that's the case, you'll be ready to read my investing chapters and keep growing your money.

Nest Egg - *Another name you may hear in regards to savings is **nest egg**. It's just another way of referring to money saved for emergencies. You'll continue to build up this*

nest egg throughout your life. As you enter different stages of life, your savings goals will
change and as well as your reasons for saving. While you're in high school, aim for $5k,
and if that's too easy, don't stop and start investing that money (see chapters 10 and 11).

Giving/Tithing

Another important part of your budget is giving or tithing from a Christian
perspective. Giving is important because you're learning how to live on less
money, adhere to your budget, and practice financial intelligence. Succeeding
in this means you have the ability to bless/help those around you. From a
Christian point of view, we know this is standard practice. But, even from a
non-Christian perspective, it can be impactful to make giving a standard part of
your budget. This can be as simple as giving a large tip to a waitress you know
is working hard. Or you can be the saving friend that comes to the rescue at a
friend or family member's time of need. Think about the positive impacts you
can make, especially as your finances grow overtime. Having a generous view
of your money is the next step in the concept of living on less.

Adding giving to your budget can be easy too. The standard view of tithing
is 10%, which would be an additional 10% you're setting aside for this specific
purpose. You can even have a generosity budget in addition to this; the point
being - determine an amount of your budget you can use for your acts of
generosity. You can even set aside that portion of your budget, allowing it to
grow in your savings account if you want to have a larger sum of money for an
act later on. Imagine helping a survivor of a devastating storm or even helping
the homeless have their own home. Whatever your method, similar to what
Dave Ramsey says, you're practicing financial wisdom early like no one else so
that one day you can give like no one else[1].

Bringing Your Full Budget Together

Now you know all the parts to fully form your budget! To do all of this, we
go back to the EveryDollar app. In Chapter 1, I talked you through inputting

Here's My Paycheck! But What Do I Do with It?

your expenses and focusing on lowering them where you can, decreasing the unnecessary things you buy. This was in anticipation of increasing your income with your new job. Now, input your new income into the app along with the 10% for saving and the amount you picked for your generosity budget. You're left with an amount called your **discretionary income,** money you are free to spend. And with that, you've made your budget and know how much money you're working with each week. Just make sure you stick with it!

 **Discretionary Income -** *This is essentially money you didn't need. Bills are paid, and your car is full of gas. You've saved and given your share. This remainder is your fun money for food, dates, crappy mobile games, whatever you want.*

Let's do a brief example of what your budget may look like, using mine from sophomore year. I roughly made $80 a week from mowing, which would be $8 in savings from the 10% Rule. Then I drove a truck which really helped drink the gas at $20 a week. I'd move my money into my savings account first thing, then keep the rest in my checking and use my debit card when I needed to. This kept me with about $52 in extra/discretionary money. This was plenty to go to dinner with friends and see the occasional movie, but sometimes I didn't even spend it all or even want to. Whenever I had extra left, I threw it into my savings, too. I realized I needed a lot less than I thought, even for my fun money, so I upped my savings percentage more each week. This is something for you to figure out and is different for everyone's situation. High school can honestly be the perfect time to save even 50% if you wanted! Also remember, the more you work, like in the summer compared to throughout the traditional school year, you're going to have even more money to save. Just remember to continue inputting budget changes in EveryDollar whenever your income or costs change.

 **EveryDollar -** *Every time you buy something, plug that into EveryDollar. It will keep track of each of your expenses for whatever pay period you set up. Along with this, check it daily so you're always aware of where you are in your budget.*

Budgeting, which you'll learn more about as you get older, isn't fun by any means. In fact, it's not something that we're naturally good at as young people living in a world where every building down the street is designed to constantly give you reasons to spend money. Every sign is flashing fancy products to you with "good deals." This is why we're discussing budgeting now when you're young. The key to budgeting is building your mindset as a student to where you gradually think more about how you spend your money. That mindset will lead you to use more **self-control,** resisting the temptation to spend as well as the peer-pressure to buy things we don't need. Budgeting is something we'll continue our discussion in the college chapters and in the other volumes in this series as we both get older.

Summary

Not only are you learning, but now you're earning. Remembering the sweat you put into each of your paychecks teaches you the value of those dollars like nothing else. Every time you receive your paycheck, the first thing you do is put your 10% in the bank, building up your nest egg. You've got to work hard and get in this habit so that you're prepared for when things go wrong. While making saving a piece of each check second nature, you're learning that you truly can live comfortably on much less than you'd typically think. That is a mindset you'll keep with you well into college and beyond, allowing you to not only save, but to start building true wealth for your future and family.

Tools for the Journey

- ***Rich Dad, Poor Dad by Robert Kiyosaki:*** *Another key financial book in my life. In conjunction with The Wealthy Barber, this reinforces the golden rule of saving 10% and living on less. This book allows you to examine two very different lifestyles of people and how they manage their money. You notice a huge, positive difference for the one who restrains themselves and saves compared to the one who spends. It's a good companion when looking at the last two chapters about investing.*

- ***Google Sheets and Excel:*** *Don't underestimate the benefit of organization. In addition to your EveryDollar, you can use these tools to write out where all of your money comes from and needs to go. With them, you can notice where you may have spent money and shouldn't have. You can also input calculations to see how different percentages from each check would make your savings grow over time.*

Chapter 4: Taxes - The Basics You Need

Now comes the sexiest part of getting paid, taxes. To keep it simple, **taxes** are money collected from citizens by the government so it can run the country. Taxes are how the government gets paid. From the president, to our brave military, to the very roads we drive on and the police that patrol them, my and your taxes are at work paying for all of it. Typically, when you're paid by a business, you'll likely notice some money was missing. You didn't get every dollar you earned from your shifts. This is because taxes were taken out of your wages. That also includes your tips when you report them to your bosses. I know. It sucks, but it's the new normal we have to get used to when we start working.

Taxes are usually an alarming surprise to high schoolers working their first job, but taxes are something we all have to pay. The amount you pay is based on how much you make, which at this age isn't likely to be really high. Because of that, you won't have too much taken out.

Taxes - The Basics You Need

If you receive a physical paycheck, either in the mail or directly from your manager, you may also receive a **pay stub**. This is a slip of paper with all the details for your pay period. It tells you how many hours you worked, tips you made, total money you made, all the taxes that were taken out, and the remaining money you take home after taxes. It's helpful to keep these and see how things change from each of your paychecks and for each of your jobs. Your pay stubs are also helpful for using EveryDollar because you'll be more comfortable in knowing how much money you're likely to bring home each pay period.

You'll notice a number of different taxes listed on your stub. They're divided into two types: Income and FICA (Federal Insurance Contributions Tax Act). Income taxes are divided between Federal and State. The amount you owe for federal is currently based on a **marginal tax rate (see the Quick Buck)**. At the state level, each state determines how it calculates your income taxes. Some states have a progressive tax system, meaning you pay more taxes as your income increases. Others use a flat percentage, which means everyone owes the same percentage of taxes. As your income increases in a flat percentage system, you'll owe less income taxes. Finally, nine states at the time of writing don't even have income taxes! Yea, you read that one right, NONE! If you live in one of those states, you won't even see 'State Income Tax' on your paystub.

 **Marginal Tax Rate -** *This means that for every additional dollar we make, each dollar is taxed at different marginal rates. This is where different income brackets come into the picture, as each bracket of money is taxed at different marginal rates. Feel free to look more into this. Investopedia.com is my favorite place to learn about taxes and other financial information. One important thing to remember: because we have a marginal tax rate, that does not mean you'll be taxed more when placed in a higher tax bracket. That's a common misconception.*

Now back to FICA. FICA stands for the Federal Insurance Contributions Act, a law mandating that a portion of every American worker's income be withheld to fund both Social Security and Medicare. This is referred to as an employee payroll tax, which means half of the tax is paid by your employer and the other half is paid by you, the employee. Both the employer and employee pay 7.62% as FICA taxes.

You've likely heard of both of these terms with: Social Security being "money we receive after we get old." That's not all it is, though. Not only does it provide some income for people who are 62 or older, but Social Security also takes care of those who are disabled and provides survivor benefits to certain widowers and others meeting specific guidelines. As far as it affects you, you can expect to pay 6.2% of your income as Social Security Tax. We'll talk more about Social Security when we get to Chapter 10.

On the other hand, Medicare is specifically a federal insurance program for people who are 65 years or older, certain young people with disabilities, and those who suffer from permanent kidney failure. Medicare comprises the other 1.45% of your FICA taxes.

Now you have an idea of what to expect when you get paid and won't be surprised by having to pay taxes. I know this must be annoying to read about. I was REALLY frustrated when I learned just how many taxes there are, plus I live in North Carolina, one of the states with an income tax. Instead of frustration, there's another way to look at things, though: you're contributing to caring for people like your grandparents who've worked hard all their lives and for others who are medically disabled, lacking the ability to fully care for themselves. You're also helping the country develop, build our roads, and keep our military and law enforcement strong. Ultimately, you're helping our nation continue to thrive.

Taxes can be frustrating, but they are part of growing into an adult, learning to manage your budget, and living on less. You'll also get to join in the fun of other adults and complain about paying taxes! There's a lot to be said for that. Now, let's look at the different ways you'll be getting paid, depending on your job, and how they affect your taxes.

 **Pay Stubs -** *What's becoming more common are electronic stubs. More businesses have these along with a direct deposit system. They'll give you the same types of breakdown of your paycheck but may be totally online. Be sure to ask your boss about yours!*

W-4 Form

When you start your job working for a traditional business, one of the first pieces of paperwork you have to sign is called a W-4 Form. This form isn't something most of us are told about before getting our first job, and it may look daunting to you at first because it has language on it that doesn't seem to make much sense. It's important, though, because your employer uses this form to determine the amount of taxes they need to withhold from each of your checks. I'll walk you through this as your first one is very simple since you're a student. You fill out all of your basic information, name through SSN. Following that, you'll confirm that you're filing as a single individual. Other than that, you shouldn't have anything else to fill out. The other fields are pertinent when you're living on your own as an adult, married, and/or when you have kids. You'll also see a repeated word across the form: "dependent." This essentially means that you're financially dependent on another person whom you live with. So, you're likely a dependent of your parents and will need to check that box. Other than that, that's all you should fill-out besides maybe putting a 0 in some fields signaling you lack or don't fit into a certain description.

1099 Form

I found out about taxes when my dad let me see his paystub. He took the time to explain to me how the government was making sure to get its fair share.

The Student's Pocket Guide to Personal Finance

I didn't start off with a traditional job, as you know, but started mowing instead. Because of that, I actually didn't have a typical job with a W-4 form until my first year of college working as a student librarian.

As I got to know Tim even more, I eventually took a trip to his home, a custom cabin he built in the Vineyard Creek Estates development. Just like the name suggests, he had a creek, and more importantly, the vineyard. This vineyard was huge; 32 rows of wine grapes in the form of one total mile of vine. Part of keeping grapes in good shape is constantly pruning them, meaning cutting the majority of the crazy branches with a pair of hand clippers. This allows for the grapes to grow the way you want them, mainly straight up the wiring they're attached to, without getting out of control. It also made it easier to harvest the grapes when Tim was ready to have them processed into wine.

Tim didn't have any help pruning the vines and was pretty eager to offer the job to another member of the shooting team and me. This quickly became my main job through high school so I could quit my mowing business. My duties expanded to being a groundskeeper, doing whatever Tim needed help with. Each week, I had my routines on what to do, and the work was endless. The grapes and grass never stopped growing until winter, especially during the hot summer months. It was perfect, though, because Tim allowed me to be independent, working whenever was convenient for me as long as I kept the grass and grapes trimmed.

Part of working mostly on my own was keeping track of my hours and deciding when Tim paid me. He trusted me completely and would wait for me to come to him, usually one evening every one-two weeks to report my hours; then he'd write me a check. He paid me $10 an hour, so I tried my best to get 8-10 hours a week before getting my check.This was simply because $80-$100 felt like some serious money to me, and it made any budgeting I had to for gas, savings, and eating out seem more manageable.

Taxes - The Basics You Need

You may have had the thought in the last section or reading about Tim and the vineyard, that you don't have to pay taxes with him writing me checks or in a job where you're paid with cash. Sadly no, but I really wanted to believe the same thing.

This is where Tim handed me what's called a **1099 Tax Form** each year. A 1099 documents everything you were paid for the past year from that specific employer, which they are also responsible for filling out. Your employer fills this out for two reasons: they typically paid you with either cash or written checks, and they need to make sure they document what they paid you. You don't have to fill out the 1099 like you did for the W-4 form; you just make sure the information is correct. While you won't be paying taxes with every check you get, you'll have to pay taxes on that money in one lump sum once your taxes are filed instead of paying them gradually.

Filing Your Taxes

Every year, we have to do something called "filing our taxes" which is what all your tax forms throughout the year are leading to. This means that we gather all of our necessary documentation, showing how much we earned in income, what we've already paid in taxes, any costs we incurred due to our jobs, and any other relevant expenses, then send all of that information to the **Internal Revenue Service (IRS)**. They're the government organization that makes sure we pay our taxes. Besides collecting taxes, the IRS's main job is to make sure each of us pay the correct amount, i.e not more than we have to pay. This is why we have forms like W-4s, 1099s, and many others, so we can know exactly how much we've earned for the year, and so we and the IRS can calculate what we owe.

For each year's taxes, you must file them by April 15th, otherwise known as **Tax Day**. As you get older, you'll notice how hectic things start to get for most Americans as time nears April. For now, since it's very likely you still live with your parents, you'll file your taxes along with them. This will be either through online tax websites like TurboTax, which are fairly cheap, or through an accountant. My family and I have always preferred an accountant so we can ask questions if we need to.

With an accountant, you'll typically bring or email all your tax forms to them, and they'll start asking you several questions. You answer them all, and they will help you determine your tax burden, how much you should owe the IRS in taxes. If you file your taxes using easy to use software like TurboTax, the process will be similar, just online.

What's a Dependent? - *Again, this means you are dependent on someone else, specifically, dependent on their income to take care of you. This isn't just students but also disabled folks or older family members taken care of by their children or grandchildren. Dependents are then claimed by the head-of-household, a tax title meaning they have a financial dependent. By claiming a dependent, they are given various tax benefits. When you've moved out of your parents' house totally and are out of school, you'll be ready to file as an independent or single.*

Tax Season - *This time period officially starts January 1st of each year, leading all the way up to April 15th, which is the last day you can file your taxes. This is when the atmosphere starts to change in America, becoming increasingly hectic for most people. The earliest date you can file changes each year at the discretion of the IRS but is normally always around the end of January. Many businesses need the entire four months to get all of their taxes in order because of many factors like tracking the salaries they've paid, expenses they've had to incur, and all of the payments they've received from clients through a variety of channels like cash or credit card. For the average working American, most of us wait until the last minute to get all of our forms together, and that's what causes folks so much stress around tax season. While you're in high school and even if you're in college, your taxes won't take much work or preparation. But remember, it's always better to start early in the year and keep track of all your forms*

Taxes - The Basics You Need

carefully. This is a skill to carry with you your whole life. Filing them earlier is always better, and you'll have much less of a headache about it than your buddies!

Let's break down the process some, starting with W-4s and 1099s. The main question you should think about is, "Based on my type of job, **when** and **how** will I pay my taxes?" From a W-4 type job, where you're considered a true employee of the company, taxes are taken out of each of your paychecks. So the **when** and **how** for W-4 taxes are every paycheck, and they're withdrawn automatically for you, so there's not much you have to worry about with this one. **When** you file your taxes, it's likely you won't have anything further to pay in. Instead, what will probably happen is you'll receive a small tax refund from the IRS. This is most often the case for young student workers with W-4 type jobs.

In short, the refund comes because you paid more than what you actually owed either to the state or federal government. This is because your W-4 tax withholdings are only an estimate for how much should be taken out. Rarely would this not be the case, but it always feels like a nice treat if you do get a small refund. Otherwise, you won't receive anything and will just pay the accountant for their services. If you do have to pay in, meaning you didn't pay enough throughout the past year, it's likely going to be a miniscule amount. Bottom line, taxes for high school students aren't complicated, so you're the most likely to expect a tax refund.

With jobs like when I was groundskeeper at Tim's vineyard and where you're given a 1099, you're considered a freelancer or an independent contractor. You're not technically an employee for the company/person. Instead of paying taxes from each paycheck, you won't pay them until you file your taxes, so, our **when** and our **how**. This becomes a bit more complicated. It's going to be up to you to save a portion of each of your checks in preparation of paying those taxes. If you don't do this, there's the potential for an end of year tax bill to take you by surprise, and you'll have to pay for it out of your savings, which you aren't supposed to touch. The rule of thumb that worked for me was 10-15% additional savings from each of my checks purely for taxes.

If this seems like a pain in the butt, I completely understand, but it's yet another reason practicing your savings habits will pay off for you. This means you'll be saving 20-25% of the money you make because you know you'll have to pay the taxes on your income at the end of the year.

There are some other things we need to break down, too, because it's possible you won't technically owe any taxes at all.

Deductions

When it comes to taxes, there are an incredible number of nifty tools put into place that, if you choose and know how to take advantage of them, will heavily help you with your taxes, reduce the amount you have to pay, or increase the amount you receive as a refund. A large amount of these aren't things you'll have to worry about because you likely live with your parents and are therefore claimed on their taxes as a dependent. So, we'll touch more on them as we move into the College Chapters, but for now, we can talk about deductions.

Tax deductions are ways of deducting the total amount of income you owe taxes on. Typically, you acquire deductions by the manner you file your taxes, showing that you meet certain requirements. These are awesome because they can help you not pay taxes at all, depending on both your income and situation. There are several types of deductions, most of which aren't going to be of concern to you because you're in high school and aren't working full-time. There are still a few you can take advantage of that most students aren't aware of, the most important of which is the **Standard Deduction.**

The standard deduction is a fixed amount that Americans are eligible to claim to reduce the amount of their taxed income. In short, that means if your income, regardless of your **filing status,** is less than the standard deduction, then you will not owe income tax for that year. And, just like with income taxes, there is the Federal Standard Deduction and State Standard Deductions. Both of these are things you can research and ask your accountant about because they often change whenever there's elections. The same logic will apply though for either one: if you make less than the Federal Standard Deduction, you won't pay federal income tax and the same for the state. A rule of thumb you can normally depend on is that if you make less than your state standard deduction and don't have to pay, you'll most certainly not have to pay federal income tax. The federal standard deduction is normally much higher than any states. If you live in a state without an income tax, then this is another thing you won't have to worry about.

To find out what the federal standard deduction is or even if your state has income tax, you can look at a few places: the IRS's official website, www.irs.gov, will tell you instantly what the federal deduction is, and you'll be lead to it quickly by Googling "What's the Federal Standard Deduction?" Similarly, do this for your state, and you'll be brought to their department of revenue or similar site. When looking through these sites, the tax for a 'Single' applies to you, unless you're either married or the head of household. So, think about how much you've been paid for the year so far and what you're likely to earn for the rest of it. Are you over the standard deductions? This is another reason the EveryDollar app can be helpful to you, or at least some type of spreadsheet. You can use it to keep track of 'every dollar' you earn! Please, try to enjoy the pun, we can all use a chuckle when we talk about taxes, am I right?

Schedule C Filing

Now, there's a special case about deductions if you're working a 1099-type of job. When you file a 1099 tax form, you're considered to be self-employed and/or an independent contractor. Because of this, you have to file under something called Schedule C, meaning that your income shown will be technically considered as business income, but only for the income you earned from your 1099 based jobs. If you own your own business in the future, you'll also have to file this way showing the amount of income your business earned. Here, you'll get to see the huge benefit of working these types of jobs. You're open to a wide range of extra deductions, in addition to the standard deduction. These deductions are your work-related expenses. This means that when you buy things specifically for the purposes of using them on your job, they are tax deductible.

My vineyard and mowing jobs make for good examples, mowing especially. I had to continuously buy gas for my mower, weedeater string, and bottled water to stay hydrated. But all of those purchases were deductible from my taxable income when I filed because they were items I used specifically for my job.

Thinking about your 1099 job(s) going forward, what do you think would fall under the deductible category? As you're considering this, keep in mind that there's an exception to this type of deduction: clothing. This makes sense because then we would just deduct all of our clothing we purchase every year, wouldn't we? It would be an easy thing to abuse, and the IRS would have some insanely complicated investigations on their hands to sort out which clothes are work clothes and which are not.

Mileage

You can also deduct the use of your vehicle for work in one of two ways. You can either deduct the mileage you traveled for your job or deduct the maintenance cost of your vehicle for the year. You can write your mileage off if it fits under one or both of these terms: traveling from an office to a separate worksite or business-related location or for any driving you do on business-related errands. For each mile you drive, you deduct a dollar amount from your taxes. At the time of writing, the mileage deduction is $.56 per mile[1]. This type of deduction can really be helpful if driving is a huge requirement of your job, like Doordash or Grubhub. Every mile you drive while you're on delivery is deductible.

Which is better? *In almost all cases, it's going to be best to choose mileage over vehicle maintenance. It's generally unlikely you'd have more maintenance than mileage to deduct, but you should record both so you can make an informed decision at the end of the year. To do this, keep your receipts for vehicle maintenance expenses and a mileage log that tracks every deductible mile driven. A great app for keeping track of your mileage is Everlance. For your first official tax year, keep track of it all, so you can ask your accountant which would be best.*

So, if you're a 1099 contractor, you'll likely have some good deductions waiting on you at the end of the year. Remember, keep track of every receipt and mile you drive for work. Even if you're not sure if something is deductible or not, it's worth keeping the receipt to ask your account about during filing.

Finally, DO NOT buy extra things for work that you don't actually need just to get a deduction on your taxes. There's a common misconception spending more money to get more deductions will somehow "save" you money by not paying as much in taxes. This isn't true. Doing this in any capacity will cause you to lose money, even though you're paying slightly less in taxes at the end of the year. Remember that this is a misconception, and DON'T DO IT! Another way to think about it is this: If you could truly spend more money on deductible things and then end up making money off of the government as a tax refund, our government would be bankrupt.

Summary

I know this was an overload of information, but every student needs to know these basics about taxes. Taxes are a little different for everyone, so make sure you can identify what kind of form you'll be dealing with. Do that, and you won't have unexpected surprises. In addition, think about what ways we've talked about that you can use to save some money through deductions. For many people, there are things they need to deduct from their taxes, and they may not even realize it. Finally, continue both researching prior to filing your taxes and asking your accountant questions when you go to file your taxes. You'll be well prepared to handle your money throughout the year, and you'll know what to expect when filing your taxes!

Tools for the Journey

- ***TurboTax:*** *This is both a platform that makes filing taxes very simple, especially for students, and also explains aspects of filing taxes in ways that anyone can understand.*

- ***Everlance:*** *This app keeps track of all the work-related miles you drive without you having to worry about counting. Just tell it when you're about to travel for work, and it'll document them.*

- ***Investopedia:*** *This website could be a tool for every single chapter in this Pocket Guide. It has information on not just investing, but taxes, credit cards, and even budgeting. A surplus of helpful information is available to you from the basics to advanced. This is a tool we can all use for our personal finances for the rest of our life.*

Chapter 5: Credit Cards

Now, we can breathe a little bit after trudging our way through taxes. For the last chapter of the high school section, we're going to talk about something much more interesting: credit cards.

What Are They?

I'm sure you've heard of them and likely have even seen them be used to pay for things. We know that someone pulls out this 'credit card' from their wallet and buys something with it. It's a plastic card with some kind of power behind it. But that's likely the limit to what most of us know about them as students.

We've gone over a debit card, a way to directly pay for something right out of your checking account. A credit card is similar: there's a credit account attached to your credit card, and it keeps track of your purchases. You use this card to buy things based on a credit system represented by a dollar amount. The difference is that your credit account adds up the money you owe as compared to money leaving your checking account when it's spent.

Let's break that down. When a company gives you a credit card, they grant you a dollar amount of credit, also called your **credit limit** or **credit line.** For example, let's say they grant you a $500 line. With your credit card, you can then buy/pay for up to $500 worth of items or services. That $500 is called your **available credit**. When you purchase something with a credit card, your available credit decreases by that amount, and the credit card company or bank pays for your purchase with their money. Following this, you accrue your **balance,** which is the running total of how much the credit card company has paid on your behalf. Then, your available credit is your credit line minus your balance. Your balance represents what you owe to the creditor, but you have an extended amount of time to pay them back.

That's the basic principle of credit cards. They allow you to delay having to pay for something by having the credit card company front the money for you, and then you pay them back. It's similar to when you borrow a couple bucks from a friend because you're short on cash, or you forgot your wallet; then you pay them back later.

How They Work

There's a catch to this, though. With every credit card, you have what's called a billing cycle or a billing period. This is typically a one-month time frame at the end of which you'll be billed for any purchases you made over that billing cycle. The length of the cycle is different for every credit card, but you can expect it to be close to one month or 28-32 days. A typical example would be from the first of your current month, to the first of the next month as a cycle. At the end of a billing cycle, you'll receive your bill, likely both electronically (which we'll talk more about in a few pages) and through the physical mail.

This bill acts as your official notice of what you owe the credit card company, the current balance on your account. You're then given a **payment**

due date, usually 21-25 days after your billing cycle ends, for when that amount is owed.

The Catch: Interest

At this point, this isn't really different from borrowing money from your friend, just with a deadline to pay it by, right? But what if you don't completely pay your bill by that deadline? That's when you're hit with something called interest.

Interest acts like a penalty. You don't pay your bill on time, so then the credit card company charges you an extra fee on top of that bill. They do this in the form of a percentage called an **annual percentage rate** or **APR.** Look at the **Quick Buck** below for specifics on how this works. For simplicity, the interest fee represents a calculated portion of what you owe added to your total bill. You won't have to worry about interest, though, if you pay your bill on time. That 21-25-day period is called your **grace period**, an extra amount of time you're granted to pay off your bill. Not only do you have your grace period to pay your bill, but your whole billing cycle, too. Basically, after you make any purchase with your credit card, you'll be able to pay that purchase back two-four business days after you made it. So, at the most you could have nearly two months of time if you make purchases at the beginning of your billing cycle and, at the least, two-four business days if you make the purchase towards the end of your billing cycle without a grace period.

If you don't fully pay your balance off in time, you'll carry that remaining balance over. That's when the interest penalty will be applied. This is where things get a bit tricky. A grace period won't be given to you at the end of your next billing cycle if you carried over a balance from the previous one, meaning you'll have much less time to pay off your bill. That also means you'd be stuck with additional interest if you bought some things at the last couple of days in your billing cycle because you wouldn't allot yourself enough time to pay it before the cycle ends.

Credit Cards

APR - *This amount is different for every credit card, but easy to find in the card details either on the forms given to you when applying, have been accepted, on the company's website, and in the details of your online account. An average minimum APR is between 15.56% to 22.87%[1]. This does not mean you're instantly hit with an additional 17% of your bill if you carry over a balance. I don't want to overcomplicate things, but the interest you would owe depends on the amount of days within your billing period. If your annual rate is 17%, you'll have a monthly amount owed, or a monthly rate, calculated from the number of days in your billing cycle, which is different depending on the month. Not only does every company have a different APR, multiple types of APR, and penalties, but they also all calculate their APRs differently. If you're a math nerd and are interested, God bless you because we need folks like you for one thing, and the credit card company's formulas are available to look through. If you're not a math nerd, the only thing you need to remember is to PAY YOUR BILL ON TIME, and you won't ever have to worry about what the APR is.*

This is where the majority of folks get into trouble with their credit cards. It can be easy to lose track of what you owe and exactly how much you've bought with your card. Because of that, they'll rack up loads of interest, and it will build up over days and months, swallowing them in debt. We'll go over the prime way in which you can avoid this in a bit, so it won't be a worry to you.

Remember, the bottom line: always pay your credit card off before the due date! Don't get hit with interest!

Why Do People Even Use Credit Cards?

After explaining all of that, I know it's a good bit of information. You may also be wondering, "What the heck's the point if you could end up paying a bunch of interest?!" Believe it or not, there are actually benefits to using a credit card! The main one is building up something called **credit.** In this case credit means a history of how well you've paid your debts. Building that credit shows that you can be trusted to pay back your debts on time. The lender trusts the recipient or lendee to pay back the loaned money at an agreed upon time. This describes how our relationship works with a credit card company. They essentially pay for something on our behalf with the understanding that we will pay them back by our payment due date; otherwise we have the consequence of interest.

Building credit comes in the form of your credit score. Credit scores are calculated by three different credit bureaus: Experian, Equifax, and Transunion. Each company publishes credit reports of individuals who've borrowed money to some degree, and a credit score comes as a result of analyzing that individual's credit history. They're divided into 5 categories: *Poor* (300-579), *Fair* (580-669), *Good* (670-739), *Very Good* (740-799), and *Exceptional* or *Excellent* (800-850). Using a credit card will result in you having a credit score. Before you officially borrow money/get credit from a bank or a credit card company, your credit history simply doesn't exist, and you don't have a credit score.

How Are Credit Scores Calculated?

When a person, such as a young student like you, begins their credit history, typically through the use of a credit card, their score begins at the bottom, near or at 300. You'll be starting from scratch. The idea is that as you gradually use your card and as you pay it off on time, your credit is slowly building. We'll touch on all of the pieces that weigh into calculating the score when we discuss using a credit card responsibly.

Credit Score - *The bottom line is that as you continue to pay off your bill without being charged interest or being late on a payment, your credit score will increase. If you make a mistake, then your score will decrease and take some time to recover.*

Why Do Credit Scores Matter?

There are many reasons a credit score will matter. You're likely to first experience one of them when you move into an apartment or some kind of rented space, either in college or as a young adult. This means that you'd be paying an individual or a company who owns a building or home to live in that space. They would be what's called your landlord. Before a landlord lets you rent, they have you fill out an application and will run a couple of checks on you, one of which would be a credit check. They want to know your credit history to see if you'd be a good tenant for them. So, for example, if they viewed your history, and there's no red flags on it, meaning you've always paid your bills on time and never let long periods go by letting your interest build on your card, then they'd view you as a good choice. They would know you're very likely to pay them rent on time and cause few financial issues. On the other hand, if they notice you have had several problems with making credit payments on time in the past, they'll think you're going to have similar problems with paying rent, and probably not rent to you.

We'll revisit how apartments work in the college section when we talk about ways to save money in college and what renting/living on your own is like.

When we go to buy a house in our adulthood, we'll also likely have to borrow money, a WHOLE LOT of money because they're expensive! The bank will want to go through a very similar process as the landlord. When you borrow large sums of money from banks to make big purchases like this, it's called a loan (something we'll heavily dive into in Chapter 9). The biggest difference between loans and credit cards is that you're already charged interest when you take out a loan. You'll have to pay a percentage of interest no matter what. That's how banks essentially make money, from the interest you pay. Now, the banks use your credit score and history to determine how much interest they should charge you, or even if they should give you the loan at all. In a nutshell, the closer your credit score is to 850, the better deal you'll get, and the less interest you'll have to pay. The closer your score is to 300, the more interest the bank will charge you. If it's so low you're in the "*Poor*" range (300-579), they'll likely not even give you a loan. The bank acts this way so it has the highest chance of getting its money paid back with interest.

Finally, some employers are also interested in running credit checks on new employees. This can be for a range of reasons depending on the job, but again, it will generally be a sign of your dependability with commitments you've made and perhaps your trustworthiness.

Do I Need a Credit Card? Shouldn't I Worry About Credit Later?

In a sense, yes, you have to wait until you're 18 before you can even apply for a credit card. If you're not 18, that's great! You're going to be extremely prepared for a credit card when you are. But let's assume you are 18 or older. I think every student should get a credit card as soon as they can. Like I said earlier, it takes a long time to build up your credit score; years are put into making it good. Because of that, the earlier you begin building credit, the higher your score will be when renting your first apartment and when you're seeking a good deal on a home loan.

I don't blame you if you're stuck on the topic of interest though. It's truly a scary thing, and none of us want to pay it. That fear of accidentally paying interest, forgetting to pay your balance on time, and ruining your credit score is a huge reason why so many people either wait to get a credit card, or view it as something that doesn't really matter. I find, however, that this fear is caused by us not being taught properly how to use a credit card when we're young, so, of course, we'd be freaked out by the idea. We also have plenty of examples, the majority of Americans, who misuse their cards and rack up crazy amounts of credit card debt. A lot of folks even view interest as just a normal part of life. If we adopt these types of views, which are understandable, then we're going to be in a worse position credit wise when we hit the various milestones I mentioned earlier and are in need of good credit history.

Please, don't put yourself into any of these camps. I'm going to show you exactly how to use a credit card and how to COMPLETELY avoid these negative consequences so that you can put your fears to rest.

How Do I Apply for a Credit Card and Which Is Best for Me?

The first step is applying for your credit card. Like I said, you have to be 18 before you can do this. Then you're ready.

When you're 18, there's a good chance most of you are still students or soon to become students either through community college or in a four-year university. It's unlikely you have any established credit history. With those things in mind, I think the best credit card for you to apply for is the **Discover's Student it ® Credit Card**.

You'll find that most credit cards, especially the 'best' ones, are hard to get. They all want you to have high credit scores with excellent credit history, which are not friendly terms for students. Others, like those from bigger financial institutions may want you to have bank accounts with them or pay some type of annual fee. You'd be paying them $100 minimum per year just to have their card. Needless to say, you don't want to deal with anything like this.

This is why the Discover Student it ® is best. It allows students to begin building their credit, and it's easy to both apply for and qualify for. The application process begins by going to their website and working your way to the student card page. Just Google "discover student credit cards". There, you'll have a choice between two cards that offer something called cash back. **Cash back** means that for every transaction you make with your credit card, Discover will give you a percentage of that purchase back to you. As you can see with both cards, this essentially means that every purchase you make is discounted by 1% minimum!

The Student's Pocket Guide to Personal Finance

It doesn't matter which of these you pick, but it is important to understand what you're choosing between. With both cards, you'll get a minimum of 1% cash back on every purchase. With the Student Cash Back card, you'll have opportunities to earn 5% cash back at specific stores, which change every three months. With the Student Gas and Restaurants card, the one I went with, you earn 2% cash back at restaurants and gas stations. Also, all of your cash back is doubled the first year you have your card! I chose the Chrome Card simply because of the consistency. Most of the stores chosen for 5% cash back aren't ones where college students' normally shop, but you'll always need to buy gas and want to eat out. Overall, choose the one you like best.

Once you choose the card you want, you're then taken to a page where you fill out all of your personal information and choose your preferred card design. Make it a pretty one! Just in case some of the fields are odd to you: 'Gross Income' means the total amount of income you'd make in a year from your job(s) before taxes are taken out. Your housing payment would be your rent or cost of the dorm if you're in college when doing this. If you live at home, you enter "0." Finally, if you've followed this pocket guide, you should have both savings and checking accounts, so you'll need to enter your balances.

 **Non-Students -** *If you're not a student while signing up, you've probably decided not to go to college. No worries! It's no less important for you to sign up for your first credit card, and Discover is no less of a great option for you. Non-student versions of the same cards are available to you. There will be very little differences between that and the student card; you'll just not get a couple of the bonuses I mention next. You also have additional cards available to you that have different rewards instead of cashback. A complete list of Discover's credit cards can be found by doing a Google search for "all Discover credit cards". Regardless of the one you pick, you'll still be in great shape for taking advantage of my credit card strategy and building your credit.*

Credit Cards

After that, you should be all set and will very likely get approved for your first credit card. Since this will be your first card, your credit limit isn't going to be high. This is something that increases over time just like your credit score. It will vary depending on your answers to the application's questions. As a rule of thumb, I'm assuming you have some type of income at this point, having worked through high school, either just in the summers or summers in combination with the school year. Otherwise, I recommend you adjust your focus to both of the job chapters before pursuing a credit card.

Your starting credit line varies for each person. Five of my friends and I all got Discover student cards in college. We were basically running an experiment to see how much our starting credit lines varied. To give you an idea about initial credit limits, our income ranged from $1,000 all the way to $14,000, and yielded starting credit lines from $500 all the way to $2,000.

Once you've gone through the full application process you'll either be told immediately if you're denied (which there's almost no reason that you should be) or that you've been approved. Your approval may sometimes be delayed to a couple of days, coming in the form of an email. Then your credit card will come in the mail, and you're ready to activate it!

Using the Discover Website to Manage Your Card

After activating your card, it's time to create an account on Discover's website. This will be where you manage your whole account. You'll notice several tools available to you from here. I'll keep my explanation of what you're looking at simple, focusing on the most important pieces and letting you explore the rest. You'll see several cards on your screen, allowing you to do several things. Here you can find your "Current Balance," which lists what you owe, your available and total credit lines, and your last statement balance which helps you keep track of your previous balance if you didn't pay it off last month. Next is the "Next Payment Due" box. This is where you make all of your payments after linking your checking account to your Discover account.

There will be a minimum payment due if you allow a balance to sit on your card for about two weeks into your current billing cycle, letting you know the "minimum" you have to pay for the pay period. If you only make minimum payments, you're still being charged interest and misusing your card, so always strive to pay the balance off.

Another important link is the "View Your FICO Credit Scorecard" in the top right of your page. This keeps a historical track of your credit score, let's you know what's good and bad about your current credit history, and displays a few important metrics like total number of accounts, years of credit history to your name, and missed payments.

Extra Bonuses for Using a Discover Card

You'll also see your "Cashback Bonus." This keeps track of all your available cash back and updates every month/billing cycle. When you have available cashback, you can do several things with it. Since your checking account is connected, you can throw it in there as extra money and then move it where you want. It can be directly used to pay off portions of your balance, too. You can also create a gift card with it and ship it to your address. My uncle really liked doing this; he'd end up with a few hundred in cash back each year and divide it up into several $20 or $25 gift cards that he'd give out at Christmas. Finally, you can donate it to a long list of charities. It's a great little bonus each time it updates because it represents a lot of cash saved with it acting as your discount. Don't forget: Discover will double the cashback you earn your entire first year of using it. That bonus is delivered exactly after you've had it one year.

How about the "**Get a $50 statement credit**"? Whenever you refer a friend and they get their own Discover card, you're both given a $50 credit on your statement. It works by sending them a link (text or email is easiest) from the "Refer Now" button and they do the same application process you did. You're both paid your $50 credit when your friend makes their first purchase in the first three months of having the card. Something to note: you're not paid in cash but will have a bonus $50 on your current balance, meaning it goes directly towards paying off a portion of your balance. You can do this with 10 friends each year (which is quite a bit!) for $500 total. This is one of my favorite features of the card and why I think it's ideal as a student's first. You can get all of your friends involved, you each make bonus money, and you are all well on your way to preparing for your future. It's more than most people do or have done at your age!

Another cool perk exclusively for student's is the "Good Grades Credit." Every time you complete a semester of college with your GPA above 3.0, Discover will give you an additional $20 statement credit. This is a great little bonus for you to work toward, and you can get it once your grades are finalized each semester for up to five years, so 10 times.

How to Properly Use a Credit Card and Never Pay Interest

This is the fun part. You can actually actively use a credit card, without interest biting you in the butt, while steadily growing your credit score. It's done by mastering this simple method I started using right after I got my Discover card. In simple terms, you're going to use your credit like it's your debit card. Instead of using your debit card, you'll use your credit card for nearly every purchase. Then, on every Friday, pay off your credit card balance in full, ensuring that you never let your balance roll over to the next billing cycle.

The key to this method is not increasing your expenses. Just because you now have a credit card, don't start buying more things than you normally would with cash or your debit card. Your budget should not change, only the way in which you're paying for things. Paying your balance off every Friday will help you manage this. If you have $50 for your weekly budget, then your credit card shouldn't exceed that amount. Just like you wouldn't spend more money than you have in your checking account, you don't spend more money than you have with your credit card, that way you CAN pay it off every week. This will quickly become a habit to you, feeling like second nature.

Downloading mobile apps will help make this easier for you, too. If you haven't done so already, search for your bank's mobile app and create an online account, allowing you to quickly check your bank accounts. Then download the Discover mobile app. This way you can check your credit status, balance, and nearly everything else you'd see on their website wherever you are. I typically check my bank account multiple times per day and my Discover app two to three times per day. It only takes a few seconds and I'm always aware of how much money I have available in my budget and can easily track my credit card payments.

I'll be honest with you, it's going to feel strange at first when you do this, and it's mainly because the money doesn't instantly leave your checking account. I'm still getting used to it, and I've had my credit card for years. You have to wait a day or two for charges to be calculated on your credit card balance, and it's an increasing amount where you're used to watching your checking account decrease with each swipe. After you pay it off every Friday, it'll take until the next Monday or Tuesday before that money is withdrawn from your checking account by Discover. It feels very very delayed and can tease you into thinking you have more money than you actually have. We, meaning everyone with a credit card, actually spend more money with a credit card than we do with anything else. Likewise, we spend more with a debit card than we do with cash[2]. It's because of this feeling. By swiping your plastic, you lose that feeling of cold hard cash leaving your wallet; you're disconnected from it. This is exactly why you pay your balance off every Friday because that will most quickly and closely show your money leaving your account, and forces you to constantly keep a check on it. Don't worry, though. You can ease your way into it by maybe just buying gas with your credit card until you've got the hang of paying it off, then gradually using it for everything you buy.

Credit Cards

So, to recap this method: gradually get to the point where you buy everything with your credit card instead of your debit card. Never spend more money than is within your budget simply because things feel different with a credit card. Pay your balance off every Friday. That's it. With this you'll build your credit score over time, have a perfect credit history, and get a cashback discount on every single thing you buy.

 **Overutilization -** *Here's a warning about using your card, especially when you're starting from a small credit line. Your credit score can be heavily damaged if you have too high of a balance for too long which is called overutilization. Specifically, your score will take a hit if you've used more than 30% of your available credit and can even decrease if you're over 10%. It can be hard to avoid this, especially if you're starting from a limit of $500-$1,000, but that's why I recommend you start slow at first and pay your balance off every week. If you do those things while keeping overutilization in mind, you'll be fine.*

Dispelling Common Credit Card Myths You'll Likely Hear

- ***"It's good to pay 'some' interest on your credit card so you build your credit score quicker":*** This was one of the common theories adults told me when asking around about how credit cards and credit scores work. Just like I've been saying this whole chapter, this is TOTALLY false. If you let your balance carry over to the next month and are charged interest, not only will you NOT build credit quicker, but you'll HURT your credit score instead! This is one of the many false rumors that many people believe and one I was often told as a student. It led me to wait three years before I got a credit card. It's a myth that convinces people to misuse their credit cards and get hit with a high amount of debt. Remember, don't pay interest and spread the word to your friends and family so they can avoid this trap, too!

- ***"I'll just get a credit card later, when I need it":*** When I was talking to my fellow college students about using credit cards, this was the number 1 thing they said to me, or that they "just didn't want to worry about it yet." It stems from both not knowing how to use a credit card (being scared of interest) and not realizing how long it really takes to build up good credit. You need to start as early as you can because it's a long process. As an example, after the first year with my card using my method, I ended the year with an average credit score ~730 among the three credit bureaus. After that, my score grew at a rate of 12-15 points per year. This myth is also a bit odd in the sense that folks don't know when they "need" a credit card until they hit a roadblock where they realize they don't have a credit history and need it for various things. At that point, it's too late. Start young, as close to 18 years old as you can.

- *"It's ok to buy stuff with my card if I don't actually have the money for it; I can pay it off later":* Here's the really tough one. I think this myth has gotten more people into more trouble than we can count. We think it'll be fine to splurge a bit, that it can be a future problem. But most of us have a hard time being that responsible or even remembering that we're actually spending part of our next budget to make up for the cost now. Most of us aren't that disciplined. This is the easiest to fall victim to because again, a credit card feels like it's more or less "free" money. Plus, you technically have a 'while' to pay it off. This is why you get into the habit of checking both your bank account and credit card accounts daily. There's never a point when you don't know how much money you have, making your money all the more real to you. Combined with paying your card off every Friday, this will help you avoid falling into this trap, and if you ever need to use your card when your checking account is low, you'll have your emergency funds in your savings account for that exact reason. It should be done when there's an emergency, not to buy something that can either wait or is totally unnecessary.

- *"I should go shop at X store because Discover is paying me 5% bonus cashback on my purchases from there this quarter":* No. This will be a temptation you face, even if you applied for the card I did instead of the Cash

Credit Cards

Back Card. You may want to buy something extra, leave a higher tip, or splurge a bit because of getting cash back. You may see that Target has the 5% cash back deal for this quarter and determine you should shop and take advantage of it. No, don't do it! You'd be breaking one of the rules of our best practice: don't needlessly increase your expenses simply to get the cashback. That doesn't mathematically work out in your favor. Two exceptions to this would be if you find you really need something, perhaps you're moving and need a desk or some type of furniture, then notice Target and Walmart both have 5% cashback. Those two stores are where you want to look first. If you find what you need, then you get the 5% cash back aka your discount. If you typically shop for groceries at Food Lion, and WalMart has 5% cash back available, shop at WalMart for the majority of them this quarter, basically getting a discount and saving money on groceries. You want the cash back to work to your advantage, not to cause you to spend more money than is within your budget.

Summary

There you have it, both the proper way to use your credit card and everything you need to know about it. A lot simpler than you thought it would be, right? Like with most financial best practices, this is something that can feel slow, even tedious. But still, something that will pay off immensely for you in the future. It will be especially rewarding when you see your credit score tick up every month and your cash back increasing. In the meantime (and as you continue to read on learning more), keep practicing this method and inviting your friends to get their Discover card, teaching them how to use it correctly. Together, we can dispel the false myths about credit cards, help young people master using them at an early age, rack up tons of cash back, and continue the conversation about personal finance.

Tools for the Journey

- ***Nerdwallet:*** *A great app that allows you to view changes in your credit score weekly rather than monthly compared to the Discover app. In addition, it gives you several active tips on how to improve your credit score depending on your personal history. It also allows you to research other types of credit cards when you're ready to get a second one. Finally, it can keep track of your expenses, tell you which categories of items you spend the most money on, and show you any debt you have.*

- ***Credit Karma:*** *Another good credit card app with helpful tips on improving your credit score.*

Section Two: College

Chapter 6: Where Are You Now?

Do You Want to Go to College?

So now's the big decision. Do you want to go to college? This is something that needs to be thought about extensively. Before fully committing to a yes or a no, you need to think about what your passions are. What would you really like to do as a career or what are your dream jobs? Dedicate some time to thinking about them and write down 5-10 careers/jobs that sound awesome. It doesn't matter how crazy they sound, astronaut or archaeologist, write it down regardless. After that, write down at least three to four sentences explaining why that career sounds awesome to you. These reasons will help you narrow down where your passions truly lie. You may think of some careers you always thought sounded cool, but you have too hard finding reasons you'd like to pursue them. Erase those careers. They aren't the ones you're really interested in. After this, start researching the jobs remaining on your list. Figure out what the job requires; what education or degrees are needed, would you have to move, what's the starting pay, etc. If any start sounding really lame, complicated, or even impossible, put a question mark next to them. We don't want to eliminate them immediately, but it is important to steadily figure out which ones are looking the best to you.

Career Assessments - *Additional tools you can try utilizing in your research are career assessments. Essentially, these assessments can help you discover new fields of interest you didn't think about. Part of the assessments attempt to identify personality traits, but don't take them too seriously as they can change depending on many factors, like your emotions. I'd say mainly use the career assessments to generate more career ideas for you to research, especially if you're stuck at this step. As you go through college or even bounce the ideas off others, you'll develop clearer understandings of the career you'd like to pursue.*

Take as many notes about each career as you can, then take those to someone you trust and whose opinion you value. Ideally, this will be a parent/close family member, or a mentor that you have. Sit down with them and talk your choices through. Tell them why you wrote these careers down and explain why you would want to pursue them. Likewise, let them ask you questions about each or at least provide feedback. Keep in mind, you're not looking for this person to tell you which career to pursue; (that's your choice), but for them to help you make sure that's the one you really want. As you go through the process, it'll be much clearer which is the job you really want. It'll be the one you talk about most vigorously and smile about when discussing it. That's where you start and the earlier you start thinking about and discussing this (junior year of high school), then the more time you'll have to prepare.

What's the Next Step?

So why did we go through this process? Of course, it's important to know what you want to do and to have some solid reasons as to why. We don't want to act completely on a whim. This is especially true because most students don't know from birth what they want to be when they grow up. Many jobs sound cool, but it doesn't mean we really have a clue about what the job entails. The main reason, though, is to determine whether college is the next step for you. Too often, students go straight from high school to college without any semblance of a plan. This is in part because many of us are encouraged by our older family members, parents and grandparents especially, to attend so we can get a "good job" when we grow up. In addition, I was told often that I should go to college so I won't have the same financial struggles like my family, that college is the solution. That's honestly the reason I attended.

It's no question that this advice comes from a place of love with the best intentions behind it. However, it's actually not true and can lead many students pursuing a path they never wanted to go down. They just think it's what they have to do to be successful. It's your decision to become a college student or not. For your dreams and aspirations with your career, is a certain number of college years a requirement? If yes, then college is likely the next step. If not, then that's perfectly fine as well. There are numerous trades such as Heating Ventilation and Air Conditioning (HVAC), construction, dental hygienist, or welding, that only need a two-year certificate to start or allow you to start working from the bottom up once you graduate high school. To dispel the myth that everyone needs to go to college, many of these jobs pay very well. Money isn't the only piece either. As you'll see in the investment chapters and as a core theme of this pocket guide, there are many ways to grow your finances without having to go for the most high-paying job. Most of us don't even want to pursue those careers either. We'll touch on when to start investing in Chapter 10. The stress of them can only be handled by certain individuals.

At the end of the day, you have to balance your passions with financial stability while picking your career. You have to think about whether you want your job to be flexible or more routine, whether you want to make more money or have more free time, and if you want to work more independently or with people. An important thing to remember, though: in pursuit of your passions, make sure you still work to have your income. Some passions, like art and music, take a while to develop into financially successful careers. Here, you see the balance. Chasing passions like these without working to secure your finances can put you into a bad financial situation, potentially putting you at risk of never having a stable job. If you're intent on pursuing passions that take a while to grow, work a stable job to grow your finances. You can do that until you've honed your passion enough to move it from being just a hobby to a career. On the other hand, if you strictly pursue money over passion, you will likely burn yourself out. If all you do is work 50+ hours a week without developing your passions and hobbies, you will quickly grow to resent not only your career choice, but possibly your life.

As a bottom line, if more students were encouraged in this approach to college and career, they would be much happier, and there would be considerably less student debt in the country. You may even want to pursue a career right after high school that doesn't require college; instead of racking up debt for a degree you don't want and may not need, you can start working and earning. As you continue to work hard and pursue that career goal, you can gradually move up and could eventually get to the point where you begin your own company.

Just because this section is directed towards college students, it's all still very applicable, especially when it comes to balancing your debt and starting to invest after high school. In fact, if you're a student considering working or currently working right out of high school, you're able to build a larger investment portfolio more quickly than college students typically can. But we'll get to that later. The bottom line is this: college is not for everyone, nor is it the only correct path. It all depends on what you truly want to do with your life.

If I Go to College, Where Do I Begin Financially?

If you decide on a job or a path that does require college, then there's some things we should start discussing and will continue to dive into over the next several chapters. To start, I want to go ahead and say good job to you. From managing a savings account and credit cards, to putting in some deep thought about the next couple of years of your life, you've done excellently. You're already making adult decisions that aren't easy, and you're miles ahead of typical students at your age, and, heck, you're even being financially wiser than many adults.

Your Credit Card

Be careful not to slack on the good habits you've developed. Your credit card should continue to act as your debit card, building your cash back, pretty much for the rest of your life. Depending on how long you've been using it, you should consider requesting for your limit to be raised. In fact, consider making a request for your credit company to raise it every four-six months. With your disciplined use of your card and paying it off every Friday, you'll have months of perfect credit history, and it's likely that you'll be granted a credit increase. Remember the Discover cards that my friends and I got in college? Each of us was given surprisingly high starting limits which were around $1,500 each. More to the point, when we applied for credit increases every four consecutive months, our credit limits were nearly doubled each time.

Increasing your credit limit will allow you to cover steeper purchases and bills. While you're in college, it's likely you won't experience huge, immediate expenses other than college itself, which will have to be paid for by other means. Regardless, things can still pop up such as vehicle repairs. If your car breaks down and you need to be towed, you'll often not have the cash on hand to pay for it. You may have a few hundred dollars available in your checking account, but it's very possible that a bill like that could empty it. This is when you really get to see the benefit of having a credit card on hand. You can swipe it, and it gives you plenty of time to readjust your accounts to prep for the payment. It lets you breathe a sigh of relief while you're trying to get your bearings. This is also why you've gradually built up your savings, for when something like this inevitably happens.

The benefit of increasing your credit limit is also seen here. As I said in Chapter 5, overutilization can easily damage your credit score, especially when you use more than 30% of your available credit. You can see your score decrease 15-30 points, which I experienced with my first card. Increasing your limit helps prevent that from happening and gives you room to pay for those larger expenses without hurting your score. Overall, if you can get your limit to around $4,000-$5,000 throughout your first year or two of college, you'll be in good shape. Just remember, while one of the goals is to increase your credit limit, it doesn't mean you have more money. It means that as your bills and income increase, you can continue to pay the majority of your bills with your credit card without worrying about overutilization.

Keep Working Part-Time Jobs

Keep working until it's time to start up your first college semester and keep building up your savings. There are three main reasons for this. The first is simply so that you keep growing your savings, working towards that goal of having several thousand dollars in the bank as your **nest egg**. This is a habit you want to keep doing well into being an adult. The second is for college. Working hard and saving up for college will allow you to put a significant dent in your overall bill, and you'd likely be able to pay for your first semester or two without using all your savings. Your jobs will help you pay for smaller things like books, materials, and a good laptop too. There are several "little" expenses that can pop up during college, and this is a way of preparing for them in addition to working during college. Finally, even though typical high school jobs like slinging tacos, cutting lawns, and babysitting aren't ones that will exactly kickstart your career, they'll still have a place on your job resume and college application as valuable work experience. Weird right?

When applying for college and definitely for scholarships, both committees like to know more about you than just your grades. Part of that is what you've done outside of school, especially work. You'll have a lot of experience to write about. Think about what it was like having to cover a shift for someone who didn't show up or who called out sick. Or when that last bus full of kids unloads at Cookout 30 minutes before your shift ends, and your boss is counting on you to help. What about those clients that were disagreeable and wanted you to work for little to no money? Those are some rough times, but they taught you an incredible amount. You've learned how to work under immense pressure, how to operate as a team, and how to bust your butt at a job. Tell those stories when you're applying; they will absolutely set you apart from other applicants. Talk about what you learned and how you struggled. Show that vulnerability and honesty with your essays and applications. And don't forget to tell them about how you learned to start managing your finances. Anyone would be surprised and proud of your growth as a student because it's not the norm.

Working provides strong experiences for your resume that you can discuss in interviews and on job and college applications. Without it, your resume would be completely bare apart from some promises you're making, i.e. "hard-worker" or "strong communicator." When applying for college jobs, which we'll discuss in depth in Chapter 8, having that kind of strong resume will pretty much guarantee you a job. You would be surprised at how many students didn't work at all in high school, even in the summers. That gives you another edge.

Decide on Colleges

This is probably the biggest thing you have to decide. It's a good idea to come up with a list of four to five colleges that all have the majors you want. You'll hear most folks, including your guidance counselors, tell you to apply to all of them, and you definitely should. There's a lot that goes into a college application, and you don't want to bet on one specific college accepting you. If that dream college doesn't accept you, what will you do? You'd have to wait another year to apply. So, hedge your bets and apply to them all.

Here's an insider's scoop though: if you're a student who took high school seriously, showed up to class, worked hard on all your assignments, kept an A-B average, and didn't get into serious trouble, you have an extremely good chance at getting accepted at most colleges. The ones that remain difficult and require solid extracurricular achievement are most Ivy League universities and the most prestigious state universities. The underlying point is to do your thorough research, but don't stay up all night worrying about acceptance. The real challenge isn't being accepted but working hard and keeping a serious attitude when you start each semester.

As part of your research for top choices, you need to understand the cost breakdown. If you're certain about your choices, don't exactly let the price scare you, but take it seriously. Several colleges are jumping on the bandwagon of either free or highly-reduced tuition prices. That's definitely a net positive for students, but understand that tuition is by <u>No Means</u> the only expense you'll have. Each college has some cost-plan available for view and download, breaking down each expense that you can expect from them on your bill.

Community College

I also heavily recommend you look into reputable community colleges within your state or the state containing the most of your college choices. They cost a fraction of what a university does and still have numerous scholarships available. This is how I saved the most on college expenses, nearly $25,000.

Where Are You Now?

The strategy is to graduate with your **associate's degree**. Normally, students make the mistake of not graduating from their community college and want to transfer to a university after they've taken a few classes to save money. When you do this, colleges can pick and choose which of your credits they will allow to transfer. This means they could accept all, some, or none of your class credit if they so choose, and you'd have to retake what doesn't transfer. If that happens, you've effectively wasted time and money.

Associate's Degree - *This is a degree you receive after completing two full years (meaning 60 to 61 credit hours) of classes with a C or better, meeting all requirements, from a community college. The classes you take during this time are the classes we all have to take like math, science, English, and others. All of these represent what is referred to as gen-ed (general education courses). Even if you don't attend community college, you still take these classes during your first two years at a four-year university, after which, you begin taking classes more specific for your major. You can save a lot of money by earning this degree, then transferring to a university in the same state. Read more about lowering college expenses in Chapter 7.*

Most state university systems have something called articulation agreements. These agreements ensure that if you graduate with an associate's degree, all of those classes must transfer to a four-year university within that same state. When you transfer with an associate's, colleges within the state university system are required to accept all of your credits and also present you with a waiver for your gen-ed, meaning all of your non-degree-related classes like English 1-2, history, public speaking, etc. You won't have to take anymore gen-ed classes when you transfer and can go straight for your major-specific classes.

Beware, this is likely different for private colleges. They make up their own rules and are not directly tied to the state's education system. If you're primarily interested in attending a private school, a community college might not necessarily help. These aren't things most guidance counsellors know or talk about, so make sure you research how they accept transferring credits.

Where do I begin Financially if I don't go to college?

Keep doing the basics we discussed in the high school section. For both the soon-to-be college student and trade student, keep your financial habits. Build your credit and credit line, work towards your savings goal, and work your side and summer jobs. Things are going to be different for you in some senses. You won't be worrying about which college to go to and moving in a dorm. Your main objective really depends on what job you're wanting. For several trades, you'll need a one to two year certificate which you can acquire through local community colleges. This is still attending college, but at a much cheaper cost and for specific programs, such as cosmetology, culinary, and electrician. With careers in fields like these, you can still earn plenty of money and ensure your finances and future family are well taken care of. When you earn your certificate/license, then you're ready to start working with a group or company to earn experience. If this is part of your plan, you can further save money by living at home through community college. On top of that, continue to work a part-time job to fill out your resume and obtain strong recommendations from your bosses.

If community college isn't necessary for what you want to do, the main prospect you have for after high school is starting a job related to your field of interest. Start by going to similar businesses and letting them know you're interested by having a conversation with the manager or owner if possible. You could also bring one of your parents along to help introduce you. There's no shame in this. It can easily be a scary experience, and you may not know exactly what to ask them. Being a big introvert, my dad helped me by coming with me or bringing me into a conversation with local businessmen if there was an opportunity I was curious about, specifically when I was trying to get more yards to mow.

In your conversation, let them know about your interest first and foremost. Tell them you'd love to get into the field, whatever it is, after you graduate and want to know what advice they have. Here are your goals: learn about their application process, what a new hire's job looks like, if there's any particular experience they would be looking for on a resume (often you'll hear about them wanting to hire dependable and hard-working individuals), and if there's anything they can tell you about the business in general. In addition to this, you could even ask about internship/job opportunities for you while you're still in high school. The worst thing they could say is no, but it would be a great chance for you to gain valuable experience and prove yourself to them for an eventual full-time hire after you graduate.

This is a good process to walk through for whatever trade you're interested in, especially if it requires certification and testing to legally start. Being on the job site like with logging, construction, and esthetics or helping work the storefront like with retail, food, or autoparts all help you learn the ins and outs of the business. Pursue these kinds of opportunities by getting to know the people in the business and showing your interest. That will set you apart from the typical applicant and help open jobs for you.

Remember to humble yourself. Whether you want to begin a trade or are a college graduate, you have to be willing to start in a position that's not necessarily ideal as you build up experience. While you're at the construction site, you may be asked to help out by carrying tools, sweeping, and cleaning up the job site. Hands-on learning situations like this are a typical place to start. Some may not be as "fun" as you want them to be, but you're working towards a goal: becoming a full-time member of that business or crew and working hard for them is how you earn your way there.

Think about where you want to live

One thing to realize is that you're going to be starting "real life" quicker than college students. With that comes the decision of where you're going to live. This will depend on where you'll be working and if you'll attend community college. Living at home until you get on your feet could be smart if your college or job is close by. You'll save more money this way and can have your parents help you form a plan for your next steps. That's not ideal for everyone though, as some of you may really want or need to go live on your own. Maybe you really value the idea of being your own person, even if that means making a few mistakes along the way.

If you're ready to move out of your parents' house, I'd recommend you start looking for apartments. This will be one of the cheapest options for transitioning to living by yourself. There's a variety of options, and it's important you understand the differences. Ask your parents or other family and friends for help when you're choosing between them. Depending on your situation, you may want to rent one that is already furnished, so you'd only have to buy the essentials, like kitchen and bathroom supplies and maybe a few small pieces of furniture. For each option, see if the power bill is included in your rent payment or if it's separate, as well as any other extra bills that there may be like water or Wi-Fi. If there are, you'll need to ask the landlord how to pay each one. This shows just a bit about the decision-making process when picking the right apartment. That's why it's good to not do it alone if you don't have to. Either way, find the one you like and can afford each month with your current or soon-to-be job. Don't move into a place just if it's nice and you can't afford it.

Before you pick an apartment, schedule a tour. Make sure it's actually what you want. In addition to that, look up the reviews online. See what people say about the typical people who rent there, about noise, and partying. You want to pick a place that you'll be happy with. The next step is to sign the lease. It's essentially a document that holds you responsible for paying either the whole sum of monthly rent if you live by yourself or your share of the rent if you have a roommate. This means you are required to make sure that rent is paid. If you fail to do so, you will be evicted, i.e., forced to move out. Like with any bill, you make sure to pay it when it's due or there's major consequences. When

85

you first sign the lease, you'll also be asked to pay for your first, often second month's rent, and a security deposit. This will usually be equivalent to three months' worth of rent. Apartment complexes have this policy to ensure they have money to cover damages to the apartment, or if the tenant is evicted a few months into the lease. The security deposit is another measure that will be used if you damage the apartment in any way. If you haven't extensively damaged anything when it's time to move out, the security deposit will be returned to you. It acts as an incentive for you to be careful and as a way of covering the landlord from being out more money. So, when you're ready to sign, make sure you have the funds available to cover those up-front charges.

I want to emphasize how big this moment will be for you. You sign your name as the renter, making a promise of prompt and continual payment. You have a legitimate bill now and a new serious responsibility. You're continuously growing into a strong, young adult, and that's an excellent goal. Gradually, you need to take on more and more of the responsibility that our parents often cover for us while we're in high school and college: phone plan, car insurance, and food. You'll start paying these quicker than students since you're starting your career fairly immediately. As you build your income, those will be the next steps.

Summary

Whether you choose college or work as your next step, keep moving toward that goal of living on your own and forming into a responsible adult. This is the natural progression of our lives, and we don't want to staunch it, even though this can be scary. For my second year of college, I decided to live with my dad's brother and his wife in Raleigh, NC, which was six hours from home. This was petrifying to me. It was completely different from the home life I was used to, and I was on my own most of the time. I had to buy my groceries to pack my lunch, something I really wasn't used to doing. Self-motivation was huge, too. I woke up at 6:00 am each day (nearly impossible when you're used to sleeping in until 8:30 or 9:00) to drive an hour each way to school and come back at 6:00 in the evening. I had mountains of homework and work on top of that.

Even though this was incredibly difficult and frightening, it helped prepare me as an individual. I was ready when I moved into my first apartment with a roommate. It already felt natural. I adulted even harder by adding rent and power to my bills and had a larger space that I needed to keep clean, that I needed to take care of. I also quickly realized that I needed to learn how to cook, or I'd starve to death. More importantly, I learned what it was like to live with someone different than me, how to tolerate their quirks, but also how to work together to take care of the apartment. You'll experience a very similar path in your life, whether becoming a college student or working. Once you start living on your own, or mainly away from home, you'll start to enjoy the fact that you're more independent. Visiting home will start to feel more like a visit, and you'll have an eagerness to continue living your own life. This is the feeling of maturing, and it'll only grow stronger. It feels great to make your own decisions, even when you make mistakes. The feeling of that responsibility lets you know you're becoming an adult.

You're on a strong path with working and developing your financial foundation. Continue to work, research hard for your next steps (whether it be college or beginning a career), and take the time to plan. Consult your parents, other close family and friends, and your mentor to talk things through. Your whole way of life changes upon graduation. Tackle it head-on by thoroughly preparing! In the next chapter, we're going to discuss how to pay for college if you decide to commit.

Tools for the Journey

- **Evernote:** *This has been by far one of the most important apps in my life. It's an incredible note-taking app that you can use on your phone and on your computer. Use it to write down anything you want, budget goals, colleges and careers of interest, or even favorite recipes.*

- **Careertree.com and Collegegrad.com:** *These and similar websites can really help you narrow down the careers and colleges you're interested in.*

Chapter 7: How Much Does College Really Cost?

At this point, ideally, you've chosen three to four colleges that you think would be suitable for your major; however, there's still one thing you notice about each that makes you feel uneasy about the price tag. Up to this point, the concept of $10,000 was foreign to us, let alone tens of thousands. How are we supposed to spend or even get that kind of money when we're in high school?! Don't worry. It is a good chunk of change, but there's a lot we can do to ease the burden, if not remove it completely.

What am I actually paying for?

Let's start with a realistic breakdown of what it actually costs to go to college. The main cost you see advertised on either the brochures or websites is typically divided among three categories. The first is tuition, which is the cost

How Much Does College Really Cost?

of taking your classes. Tuition varies depending on the number of classes, which are measured in credit hours, you take each semester. The advertised total typically estimates what you can expect to pay per year: 24-30 credit hours or about eight to ten classes.

The second cost is housing. This is also an estimation because there are multiple dorms on a college campus, each costing a different amount. As a freshman, you'll commonly be limited to freshman only dorms. These tend to be cheapest, but they'll often lack amenities like air conditioning, individual bathrooms, and room space. Depending on where you'll be located climate wise, air conditioning may not be a problem for you, but the punchline is, freshman dorms are never the most desirable on campus. After your freshman year, you'll have the option of moving to the others. Some colleges like WCU, where I attended, have Honors dorms. These are more high-end dorms reserved for students who are members of an Honors College. An invitation to these comes if you were a high-achieving student with a high GPA and participated in several extracurricular activities in high school such as sports, club involvement, and volunteering. While these are likely to cost more than other dorms, being a member of an Honors College can have other benefits such as scholarship opportunities.

The last category is the fee category. In some cases, this amount can rival even that of your tuition payment. This is where you pay for services such as the campus library, technology, athletics (meaning those "free" tickets you get to attend a sporting event), textbooks, etc. These can vary between public and private colleges, too. It's important to look through this category and see how the fees are broken down.

In addition to those three categories, you'll also have to buy a meal plan. These are all different in structure among colleges and each college has several options. The commonality between them is that you're exchanging your money for one or more types of meal "currency" that you use to purchase campus food. You can use portions of your plans to purchase snacks and other food as well. Some portions of a meal plan can only be used in the campus cafeterias and restaurants, while the others can be more broadly used in those places as well as on campus convenience stores. In the next section, we'll talk about choosing the most efficient meal plan for you.

Ways to Save Money on College

AP Classes and Dual Enrollment Programs

There are a few ways you can save money before even going to college. The first of these is AP (Advanced Placement) classes. AP classes are very difficult classes, likely the most difficult you can take as a high school student. You'll find them across all basic subjects from advanced maths and sciences to history and English. All of these being gen-ed courses you'd normally take your first two years of college. By taking them, you're meant to be exposed to college level curriculum as well as challenging homework and projects. Typically, AP classes have the ability to increase your weighted GPA further above the possible 5.0 from Honors classes if you receive an A in them. The real attraction to them comes in the form of a standardized AP test at the end of the semester. These tests are graded on a scale of 1-5, and, depending on how well you score, you will receive college credit for the college equivalent of that AP class. So, you can enter your first year of college with several credits if you pass some AP classes, saving you time and money.

This may surprise you, but I want to dissuade you from taking these classes. Having taken many, myself and with many friends who've done the same, they're ultimately not worth it. AP classes are often FAR harder than taking the courses in college, and they can cause you a tremendous amount of undue stress as a high schooler. Additionally, the tests can be even more difficult than the class itself. While passing those tests only means you have to score a 3 or better, that doesn't mean the college will accept that class as an A. This means that if you scored a 3 on AP English for example, the college you're applying to may accept that credit, but only as a passing grade of a C. Again, AP classes are more trouble than they're worth.

A much better alternative to AP classes is taking online college courses through a dual enrollment program in your high school. Many high schools have relationships with their local community colleges that allow their students to take gen-ed classes for free in an online format. Check if your high school has a program like this. Taking classes like English 1 and 2 this way is usually much easier than the AP equivalent. You could take two or three classes without being smothered by a heavy workload and knock out a semester or even two semesters of college while still being in high school! Pairing this with finishing your associate's degree at the same community college after high school would save even more money.

Public Over Private

Generally, I would always recommend attending a public/state college over one that's private. The simplest reason for this is the overwhelming cost difference. Private colleges tend to be three to four times as expensive in nearly every facet. Broadly speaking, private colleges aren't worth the extra cost, but they have to charge an exorbitant rate because they don't receive state support and funding. They have to raise the vast majority of their money on their own. At public college, you'll be able to manage your expenses much more easily, and will have a strong shot at graduating without much or any student debt. The same can't be said for a private one.

You don't have to automatically rule out private colleges, but make sure you have a strong reason as to why you want to attend. The two biggest appeals are the small size of the institution, which necessarily carries over to a small and personal class size, and then specialty interest and/or majors. Don't go purely based on the class size, as several public colleges can provide the same experience if that's your preference. If you're interested in some specific lines of work, such as archaeology, highly-focused engineering or computer science, law, linguistics, scientific research, etc. then private colleges are more worth considering. Many of them have specialties for the entire college. For example, Harvard is built strongly around business and law, while Massachusetts's Institute for Technology is highly focused on computer science, AI, robotics, etc. If you have strong grades, big dreams, and a high-caliber work ethic, going down the specialty path could really pay off for you.

That being said, be sure to not go to a private college for its specialty if you can save most of your money and get a comparable strong education from a public college. Research the prestige of each college, as in, how your degree would be regarded by businesses in that industry of interest, their accreditations, and the general backgrounds of the faculty and staff. There's a lot to be found from this, and it can keep you on a smart track. One example in NC would be Lenoir-Rhyne and NC State. Both have strong engineering programs, but Lenoir-Rhyne is private. Furthermore, NC State has access to much larger funding, giving it access to more technology and resources and is typically more highly regarded. Finally, NC State is less than half the cost of Lenoir-Rhyne. In this case, it's hard to not heavily recommend NC State over Lenoir-Rhyne in nearly all cases. Use similar reasoning when making your decision.

Lastly, depending on your interest, you may have a difficult time finding a public college with your major. While nearly all of them offer majors extending into most subjects, more specific majors are often missing. Lisa, a close friend and recent newly-wed of one of my closest friends, Cody, attended Gardner-Webb in NC for just that reason. No other NC colleges offered degrees in photo-journalism or American Sign Language when she was applying. Gardner-Webb had developed programs for both, so it was the perfect option for her, even though it was more expensive. She got to pursue the majors of her dreams with a strong network of professors and internships, while also not being far from her then fiancé and from home.

Choosing A Meal Plan

This can be overwhelming because there are several to choose from. If you go straight to a university as a freshman, I recommend you pick a meal plan in the middle of the options available. You assuredly don't need the largest plan, which is typically an unlimited meal plan, and you don't want to just pick the smallest out of frugal instinct. You could easily run out of meals if you squander it. That's just to say, you have a limited number of meals available to you, so you want to be careful when buying food. You especially want to be careful when it comes to other stores on campus. This could be coffee cafes and convenience stores, all designed to supply you with snacks and extra things. But more importantly, they will quickly deplete your meal plan currency. Do your best to stay away from them your first year. Practice caution with your meal plan your freshman year, focusing on your three meals with a few snacks thrown in. Throughout that year, you'll obtain a better picture of the size of meal you need and how to balance it. You want the results to be you buying the smallest meal plan each year you live on campus that you can live comfortably on without spending wads of money on food you don't need.

Textbooks

You'll need textbooks for the majority of your classes, but you may notice a decline in that requirement after you've completed your gen-ed. Most colleges include a "book-rental" fee under the fee category of your bill, which can range from hundreds to over a thousand dollars. The perceived benefit of this is that you don't have to outright "buy" each of your books, as you can rent them from the campus bookstore. Beware, though, you'll run into situations where you'll still have to buy or rent certain books depending on your professor's requirements. If you find yourself in the situation where you have to buy your own books, it's best to NOT go to the campus bookstore. You'll notice that the vast majority of products sold there, from pencils to binders, are ridiculously overpriced. Online book retailers are going to be your best friends here to get the best deal. Chegg and Amazon were my favorite, and they saved me hundreds of dollars a year. Buying or renting the ebook version is even cheaper. The easiest way to find your class's books is by searching using the ISBN, which will be on your class syllabus.

Community colleges typically ask you to just purchase or rent textbooks from their campus store. Some bookstores will offer to buy back those same textbooks, but at a heavy discount of 50% from the store's sale price, of course. Because I was able to find mine cheaply on Amazon, I made a small profit selling them to the bookstore. You may be able to do the same.

Living Off Campus

While you almost always have to live on campus your freshman year, you don't have to after. This is where you can save a tremendous amount of money in a variety of ways. The chief of these is that paying rent for an apartment is often going to be cheaper than the high housing rates of your college campus. You can take further advantage of this by living with roommates. The more people you live with, the less you'll pay in rent. Ideally, you can discuss this with friends you'll make during your freshman and sophomore years and create a good group to live with.

When choosing where to live, look for an apartment that's close to campus if you can. This way, you can use the bus/tram service if it's available at your college, and you can have the option to walk, bike, or skateboard to campus. You'd be able to save gas this way, and more importantly, save yourself from having to buy a yearly parking pass for hundreds of dollars. If you have to live a bit further away from campus, you can carpool with your buddies, each of you chipping in on the cost of one parking pass.

How Much Does College Really Cost?

Cooking

Another real advantage of living in your own apartment is that you're completely in charge of your food situation, which can be both a blessing and a curse. This was something I was ill prepared for because I quickly realized I needed to learn how to prepare food besides frying eggs and bowls of cereal; otherwise, I'd starve to death. This is where learning to cook can come to your rescue like it did for me. Cooking grants you the ability to both eat healthier than with campus food and save hundreds of dollars a month. The secret to savings is when you buy your own groceries. A good rule of thumb when shopping is to stick to the outside of the isles. This is where you'll find fresh produce, meat, eggs, and dairy. Think of the typical grocery section of Wal-Mart. The inner isles are where you'll see more snack-based goods, a majority of which are unhealthy and can consume your grocery budget. On top of this, look for local fruit stands. Fruits and veggies are already cheap, but you'll find an even better deal from a local farmer. You're also helping that farmer sustain their business to bring you more food next season.

The other key to saving with cooking is leftovers. Leftovers are absolutely magical. This is how you turn your one meal into four meals for the week. You'll likely figure out it's hard to cook for yourself on a budget without having leftovers. In light of that, I recommend looking for recipes like one pot meals and pasta dishes that do just that. For example, one of my favorite meals is stir-fry. All there is to it is meat, rice, a bag of prepared veggies, and my selection of sauce. Just with that alone, I could easily make four meals a week. Combining that with basic breakfast food, fruit for snacks, and sandwiches for lunch, I would pay at most $70 a week on food. That's not bad when thinking about an average price of $9 or more per meal on your campus.

Figure out what things you want to eat and look up cheap recipes on how to cook them. That will act as your starting place as you adjust to living off campus, and you'll start to pick up tricks along the way that make cooking a more comfortable process. You can even ask your roommates about cooking together. That will reduce your grocery bill even further.

Keep Budgeting

It's time to update your EveryDollar because your bills will be changing when adding monthly rent, groceries, and transportation. This is when you'll really start learning to live on a weekly budget like we've previously discussed. You want to work to find a weekly amount you can both live comfortably on and that is enough to cover your bills. Along with that, continue your saving and giving practices. In Chapter 10, I'll explain investing as college is going to be an ideal time for you to begin that process. Lastly, you want to add the cost of each semester because you're going to work to pay your way through college.

Summary

I would argue that college is when you may experience the largest temptation to not follow your budget. The cause of that is peer pressure. While you felt gradual freedom through high school, there's an exponential jump in college. For the most part, especially when living off campus, you're an adult on your own. With this freedom comes the temptation to spend your money on a LOT of things. This can range from eating out several nights a week to partying. The bottom line is you'll need to practice **self-control** while you're there. Despite there being fun aspects to college, it's probably the most serious thing you've done in your life up to this point. You want your focus to be on earning your degree, building your investments, and most importantly, paying your way through college. You don't want or need the added worry of overspending your budget and not being able to pay your bills.

How Much Does College Really Cost?

 **Self-Control:** *This is something we have to continuously learn how to do, no matter how old we are. This is because it's hard. It's hard because it's literally the active practice of restraining ourselves. We can't go and commit acts of self-control. We have to pause and analyze the choices we've yet to make and the actions we've yet to take. The key to it is for us to utilize the power of saying "no." When we feel that temptation to break our strong financial habits, we refuse.*

While your bill will have to increase, so will the need for you to work in college. Remember, the most basic financial choice we have in life is to either reduce our expenses or increase our income. We've touched on plenty of ways to reduce your expenses, and next, we'll look at all the ways to increase your income. College will force you to do this, but it's a good thing. If you keep going and work hard, not only are you going to continue your financial journey, but you can pay off most, if not all, of your college bills. You're going to be so much further ahead than most students your age, and it's just the beginning.

Tools for the Journey

- ***Chegg:*** *Not only a good website to use for study tools through your classes, but you can also find cheap ebook rental options for textbooks you may need. Sometimes, this can be a cheaper option than finding a used physical version on Amazon.*

- ***Crock Pot or Instant Pot:*** *Potential birthday gifts that could help you save a lot of money making delicious one-pot recipes. Remember leftovers are the key to keeping a low grocery budget.*

- ***Apartments.com:*** *Perfect for helping you find the best apartment deals in the area close to your college. Use it to diligently shop around for the best apartment deal. Try to stay close to campus so you can bike or walk, and try to find one that includes a washer/dryer.*

Chapter 8: How Do I Pay My Way Through College?

How to Pay Your Way

Before you begin each semester, the bill must be paid. You pay to attend college, not pay because you have attended. You have three main options to pay your way through college: scholarships/grants, working, and loans. We'll examine each of these in their respective order, and I'll tell you everything I've learned as a recent graduate to help along the way. For most students, paying for college becomes a combination of all three options to varying degrees, in addition to support from their family.

**Please Note: I'm writing these under the assumption that you're paying for college independently. I definitely understand some students may not even have to worry about paying for college due to family trusts or that their bill is significantly reduced thanks to family. Under this assumption, then any extra help with your college will be just that, extra. You're planning and acting like you'll pay for it yourself, which means you won't have to depend on others for their support. If you get any support outside of these options, sweet! You'll be all the more at ease when paying your way.

Scholarships and Grants

Scholarships and grants are what I call the "Free Money." It's money given to you exclusively for college use. Typically, they'll be in the form of a gift from groups like good-hearted families or companies, the colleges themselves, or from the state and Federal Governments. Scholarships, grants, and even loans will all be allocated to you by your college in what's called your **financial aid award**.

 **Financial Aid Award -** *This is a section each college will have for you to access in your account page through their website. This helps you keep track of your funding, your official college expenses, and any messages from the Financial Aid Department. It is also where you accept all financial awards (scholarships to loans), so check it frequently for updates from your college. You have to either accept or decline every financial award you receive before the start of each semester so be sure to remember that! Finally, this may be where you pay your college bill at the start of the semester. To do that, look for a button or area that says something like "Pay My Bill."*

There are two types of scholarships. The first, **merit-based**, are ones awarded to students with high achievements, strong grades, work experience, and volunteer experience among other things. In other words, merit means you have to earn them. These are the most difficult to win and usually give students a lot of dread. That dread comes from the in-depth application and having to write an essay on an obscure topic. I'm definitely with you there. Before I even began writing the essay I felt like I didn't have a shot. I hated writing. While

How Do I Pay My Way Through College?

that's a relatable attitude, it's one you have to push through; otherwise, you'll convince yourself to not apply for them.

Essay writing tends to be the most difficult with the first few scholarships you apply for. Each usually revolves around similar topics such as diversity, a challenge you had to overcome, or your reasons for going to college. Whatever the topic, the key to writing is to be honest and open up to the reader. The topics all revolve around one true thing, YOU. The readers are genuinely interested in who you are and the uniqueness your story brings. Despite how you may feel when writing about your experiences (I always felt like I didn't have anything to offer with my story aside from liking to play video games, marching band, and running cross-country), remember that your story is interesting. Many students make the mistake to try and create a story that sounds interesting. Instead, just tell the reader about yourself, your goals and aspirations with college to simply your hobbies. That's exactly what they want to know. You're perfectly interesting.

The other types of scholarships are **need-based.** These are awarded to students who are more financially in need than others. Compared to merit-based, less information is given when filling out these forms, but sometimes you'll still have to provide some details such as your hobbies, sports you play, and other interests. Occasionally, there are essays as well, but they are not the main determinant in the student given the award, but they are helpful if deciding between the front runners for the award after their financial need has been considered.

Your financial need is determined by filling out the **FAFSA (Free Application for Federal Student Aid)**. You complete it with your parent/guardian and document both of your incomes, savings, tax status, etc. Completing the FAFSA is a requirement to attend college. The result is a federal form that determines, through estimation, the expected contribution from your parents to your college cost, as well as the amount of aid you're eligible to receive from the Federal Pell Grant, which we will look at in a bit. Colleges and other entities use this form to establish the financial need of students and their families. This keeps everyone honest.

Key Advice

That's the simple breakdown of each type of scholarship, but there are a few other key things you need to know. **First and most importantly,** apply for as many as you can because you can't guarantee which ones, if any, that you'll get. Most scholarships aren't full rides to college, but are one time payments of $500 to $1,000. Every little bit helps, but college usually costs much more than one or two scholarships. You have to be resourceful, always looking for scholarship applications as a high-school junior and senior. High-school guidance counselors will start sending scholarship applications to seniors either in the summer or as their last school year begins. These will mostly be local and state scholarships. Apply for all of these if you can as most of them will be high award amounts at the state-level. Bearing that in mind, that's also the reason they can't be the only ones you pursue. The competition is fierce for them, and you know if your guidance counselor sent it out, others are certainly doing the same at their high schools.

This is where you have to use the Internet, starting with your college. Once your FAFSA is submitted and you're accepted into a college, you can start applying for that college's scholarships. Check to see if they have a mass application form, as in, one that automatically applies you to dozens or even hundreds of scholarship funds from the college. It applies to scholarships that best fit criteria you fill-out on the scholarship form, such as your intended major, your hobbies, and the county you're from. After that, look for other scholarships that aren't included in that form. Search for any that are specific to your field of study, sports you play, Honor's College and any others you may qualify for. In addition to your college, look for state-level groups or scholarships sites, too. These may even overlap with websites you came across from going through your counselor's emails.

To broaden your search, you can use sites dedicated to scholarship applications like Scholy.com. Some of these, Scholy.com included, have small subscriptions for their services (only $1 or $2 a month), but they are well worth it. They allow you to browse through thousands of scholarships that you are most likely to qualify for. At this point in the research process, you've probably noticed one very annoying thing: scholarships can be very specific and VERY hard to qualify for. I've seen several that drill down to exact goals and dreams, or the county you grew-up in. I know that really brings on feelings of discouragement and you feel like you're not qualified for anything. That's not true!

A secret about scholarships is that there are thousands of them waiting to be applied for, plenty you meet the criteria for. But it does hammer home why it's essential to research and apply to more every day. Make a goal for yourself, something simple like applying for at least one scholarship a day. Let that be the practice you fall into starting your senior year in high school. This will allow you to apply for many before you know it, heavily increasing your chances of winning them, all while keeping up with homework and the fun of senior year.

My second point goes along with the first. Students are hit with more emotions than we realize when dealing with scholarships. Chief among these is negativity, which we use to convince ourselves we won't get the scholarship, often before we've even applied. It may show up when explaining your hobbies or when you're writing the essay, or just when you're exhausted from browsing through so many. Don't let this overwhelm you, and more importantly, don't let this emotion prevent you from applying to them every day. Don't tell yourself, "I've applied for a few. That's enough. If I get 'em, I get 'em." You're not the only one to feel overwhelmed. In fact, most students don't even apply for scholarships because of that feeling. They assume other kids who are "smarter" or more "popular" will get them instead. Not applying and miniscule digging to discover scholarships causes hundreds of them to go unapplied for each year. It's literally free money students talk themselves out of applying for! Remember that when you're using directories to find scholarships that may be obscure. Apply for as many as you can! It's your chance to take advantage of the many ones that are out there.

There was a guy in my class named Mitch who really took advantage of this idea. He set a crazy goal for himself by applying for two scholarships a day. It blew my mind thinking about how he could even find that many. He took advantage of all the avenues I've mentioned, especially searching through directories, but there was a step he added in the process that I was honestly against. He literally applied for every scholarship he came across, despite not meeting the criteria for most of them. He didn't lie about any of his information either. It didn't matter if the scholarship focused on minority education, girls-only, or even major-specific requirements. He applied for them ALL. This seemed like a waste of time to me, a person who would dig and dig trying to find the perfect scholarship for me, that is, until he said how many he was actually awarded. In total, he received over $100,000 in awards!!!

Stunned, I learned just how powerful applying en masse truly is. I remember one scholarship in particular our guidance counselor sent us from a pet rescue organization; it was for $1,000 and was specifically for students who had immediate relatives employed or previously employed by the rescue group. As none of the students in my class fit the bill, we all ignored that one, all of us except for Mitch. His family had never even heard of the organization, but he applied anyway. He got it simply because he was the only one to apply! Let this be an example to you as to why you apply for nearly every scholarship you come across.

How Do I Pay My Way Through College?

My third and final point is about scholarship applications themselves. Local scholarships will normally require a mailed, written application, while the others you find at the state level and through directories will primarily be online. You have to be serious and very careful when filling out written forms. First, use a pen to keep the form profesional. Don't use pencils. Fill it out slowly; you don't want to have a bunch of mistakes and stray ink marks. Make sure all of your information is correct. More importantly, though, are the directions for each scholarship. Almost all of them have particular form requirements unique to each. Some have you write your essay in the form of a letter, ask you to mail in a specific kind of envelope, or ask you to staple your resume to the front of the application rather than the back.

Insignificant stuff, right? These are actually ways to weed out applicants that don't take enough time to follow directions. Scholarship committees are tough on the applicants and will throw away your application for those seemingly "minor" mistakes. It doesn't matter if you wrote a tremendous essay or have crazy high grades, they'll throw it away without reading it. This helps them narrow down the winner and encourage applicants who are serious enough to read all directions. There were several applications I messed up because I just hurried through them. Take your time with each one and make sure you read the directions!

With your essays, the first five to ten you write will likely cover different topics, but you'll soon find that essay topics are widely repeated. You can use this to your advantage by reusing them. You may only have to alter a few sentences or paragraphs to specifically address the audience. Here's a few of the topics I've run across The most while applying: "How Would You Define Diversity?"; "What Would This Money Mean to You?"; "Why Do You Want to Major in *Your Major Here*"; and "Talk About One of the Most Memorable Experiences in Your Life." These are umbrella topics which can be more specific and often will be. Nevertheless, you'll be able to borrow from each essay to consistently make solid scholarship applications.

Grammarly and Proofreading - *Before calling your essay "finished," I highly recommend you upload it to Grammarly. This is a fantastic website that performs several grammar and spelling checks on your content. Not only is it helpful for your scholarship essays but for anything you have to write. I've used it countless times while writing your Pocket Guide! You can also take a few of your scholarship essays, especially the ones you're really unsure about, to a trusted English instructor to proofread. It's amazing the improvements you can make with having another person read your content. After staring at your paper for too long, you can easily miss things that a fresh pair of eyes can catch.*

Grants

The **FAFSA** is the main form required for grants. In this sense, grants are government funding, either state or federal, given to you based on your financial need. They come from a limited pool of money, so make sure you complete your FAFSA as soon as possible. You start by making your account at fafsa.gov with your parents, then answering all of the finance questions. This is a fairly lengthy process and very confusing the first time you do it. It's imperative to make sure all of your financial information is in order before you fill it out. Most colleges have professionals in their financial aid office to help you through the process and so do many banks/credit unions. In addition, you can visit your accountant who can help you and your parents complete your FAFSA. I highly recommend either one to help explain some of the process. After the first time, it'll feel much easier for your following college years. Once you submit your FAFSA, there will be a small waiting period for processing, usually around one week. You'll get an email saying they're finished, and you can then view your account. You're waiting to see how much funding you qualify for in the form of the Pell Grant, which will be the amount shown. This comes directly from the Federal Government in payment to your college at the start of each semester and is calculated primarily by your parents' total income. The higher their income, the less grant money you'll qualify for because your parents are expected to contribute a certain percentage of their income to your college bill.

In all transparency, there are some issues with this system. One is that siblings aren't properly taken into account by the formula, especially if they're also attending college. That can severely decrease your awarded aid. It's not realistic to expect a household that makes $50,000 per year to contribute 10% of that each year to three college students' education; however, that's the nature of the beast. It's hard to complain about free money, regardless of the amount, but it's something you need to be aware of.

One of the last steps to your FAFSA is choosing the colleges you want to receive it. They'll then receive an electronic copy form FAFSA.gov with your information. It will be used by both the college and the state to determine any other grants for you. If your state has an educational lottery fund, a variable portion is likely to be allocated to you. Some colleges, with a strong emphasis on some, will give you a free "grant" or "scholarship" automatically based on your financial need. Even if each of these amounts are small, each chunk adds up.

There's a small warning about scholarships offered to you from colleges, specifically private colleges. During your senior year, you're going to get a ton of emails. And I mean, a TON. A portion of them will be about scholarships and information from your guidance counselor like we've already discussed, but others will be from colleges enticing you to apply and attend. I promise you, this will get to be extremely annoying. They mainly come from private colleges as huge marketing campaigns begin. If you receive emails from public colleges, or if you're mega-smart and sent your SATs to an Ivy League

University, chances are those are more of a priority as you don't receive nearly as much junk mail from them. Private colleges will hit you with plenty of what I call "awesomeness marketing," meaning they'll tell you all about why they think their school is awesome, their professors are awesome, and just how awesome you are if you attend. They'll finally, and very often, hit you with a scholarship offer for you to attend. It'll sound good, too, possibly in the $10,000 range.

A friend of mine from high school, Megan, received one such email from an engineering college in NC, called Lenoir-Rhyne-- as did most of the 100 in my graduating class. Megan was swept away by the awesomeness and was nearly sold on the fact that they offered her, surprise surprise, a $12,500 scholarship!! "Wow! That's gotta be close to like, two years of free college!" she shouted. All of us thought she'd hit the jackpot, only to see a completely different story once we started looking through Lenoir Rhyne's website. A quick Google search revealed that, before any aid, the estimated cost was a little over $52,000, per year! Megan's scholarship wouldn't even put a dent in a total of $208,000 for four years. Needless to say, she decided not to go. Make sure you do significant research if you get emails like these. Private colleges tend to offer some kind of scholarships like this to most prospective students as a way to lure them in and make it seem like significant money is being saved. In reality, you'll almost always be paying much more than for a public school.

Why Should I Work in College?

As I said earlier, we need to treat college very seriously. Not only is it serious for its educational time commitment, but it's the most serious financial move you'll have made up to this point in your life. It's expensive to go, and because of that, so many students become plagued with insane levels of debt that follow them for years after college. They often don't realize just how much money they'll lose because of it. The most sure fire way for you to avoid debt is to work in college. Working is what allows you to pay your way through the

How Do I Pay My Way Through College?

whole thing and have the potential to come out debt free. Having a job in college is tough and adds a lot to your schedule, but it's infinitely better than taking out loans. After you graduate, you'll be glad you did.

It's important that you continue with the work ethic you created in high school and look around for jobs after you've gotten adjusted. Entering into college is a huge transition unlike anything you've ever done before. In high school, your day was well planned out for you: have breakfast with your friends around 7:30, classes from 8:00-3:00, and then the day was over. You had a solid structure to your academic life with few changes. College puts you in charge of your schedule. You pick exactly what classes you want and when you want to take them. Generally, you'll take four to six classes and attend them every other day. Apart from that, it's completely up to you how you spend your time for the rest of the day. You have sole responsibility for everything you do. The magical fairies that used to change your toilet paper and do the dishes are no longer around and no one is there ensuring you go to class or finish your homework.

To help you adjust, figure out where the best places to do homework are, what food isn't terrible, and which professors you want to avoid at all costs. After a few weeks, you'll soon realize you have a lot of free time on your hands. That free time is one of the most important things about college. It's something you can use to be incredibly productive, but it does take some drive. College is even better than high school for growing your finances. This is in part because most of your expenses were paid before each semester, which we will discuss later in the chapter about college loans and debt. Typically, that money secured your housing, meal-plan, and access to most campus amenities in addition to tuition. Aside from those initial payments, your day-to-day expenses are little to non-existent (assuming you keep resisting the Starbucks temptation, of course). You can save most if not all of the income you'll earn, but it's also nice having a little extra spending money if you want to eat off campus or watch a movie. Chances are as a first-year student, you're living in a campus dorm without being allowed a car, or, if it's anything like WCU, you're allowed a car but must park it miles away in the Freshman Lot. Because of this, the best place to begin your job search is on campus. After you've moved off campus or started your second year, you can then even search for jobs in local towns. For those, apply the same techniques we used in Chapter 2.

Searching for On-Campus Jobs

Apart from asking around, the easiest way to find jobs available is through your college's job portal. Like paying your bill and financial aid, this will be accessible from your college's website. After you log-in to your account, look around for a section that says "Jobs" or "Job Portal." It could also be listed under a mascot inspired name like WCU's JobCat. This displays all job listings on campus with fairly detailed descriptions. Generally, there's two categories of on-campus jobs you'll see: work study and student worker jobs. For both, you're only allowed a certain number of hours, 20 at the time of writing in 2021. **Federal Work-Study positions** are granted to you based upon your FAFSA. The higher your financial need, the higher the chances you have of being awarded work study funds. This will function and count as a grant except it will be paid through the means of paychecks rather than a lump-sum. Since it's considered a grant, you'll also have to either accept or decline the funds on your financial aid award. Here are the key things to know about this category:

- There is no minimum or maximum amount of money you could be awarded, but the average award is $1,808 annually[1]. Once your FAFSA is processed and viewable to you, any work study money you've been awarded will be indicated.

- You can't earn more than the award package. When you've been paid the full amount for the semester/year, then you can no longer work as a work study. Seldom is there an exception to this rule, but you may receive additional funding if other work study students in your college won't work all their hours.

- Your hourly rate will vary depending on the specific job and location but cannot be lower than current minimum wage. For example, I worked an identical librarian job between two community colleges in my first two years. For the first, I was paid $7.25 per hour (minimum wage at the time) at the small-town college, then $9 per hour starting at the community college in Raleigh, a capital city.

- It's possible to receive raises each year as a work study, but that does not mean you'll be awarded more grant money. You'll just have to work less hours to get it.

- There are also **State Work-Study programs** which function similarly. The funding comes from the state rather than the federal government. Research to see if that option is offered by your state and see if you could get better funding through one.

Part-time student worker positions are directly funded by the college. They encompass the majority of campus jobs:

- They're not restricted to students based on financial need like work study positions.

- You're paid from the department you work for and have a higher chance of receiving raises since each department has their own pool of money. This also means that you will typically retain your job through each semester unless you have a poor performance.

- There will be a wide variety of jobs to choose from. Because of this, you'll have a better selection of positions and a wider range of starting wages compared to work studies.

My Advice - *Work studies can be solid small jobs for your first year of college, but I wouldn't pursue them much after that because you can make more money working as a part-time student worker where you're paid by the college's funds. As a part-time student worker, you won't have the same pay limit hanging over your head as a work-study student. Whether federal or state, work-study raises are hard to come by because you have a limited money supply, and your supervisor may be hesitant to give you a raise because that might mean you'd work less hours for them. Finally, work studies tend to go away very quickly. Students aim for them first, making them surprisingly competitive. One benefit in being granted federal funds is that you can market yourself to your professors as "free labor" since they wouldn't be paying you from their budget. You can use this to your advantage and potentially have them create a paid position that's very relevant to your career interests. This would essentially lead to the creation of a paid internship position for you that would be good career and resume experience.*

Narrowing it Down

For many students, we don't know exactly what we want to major in when we get to college. If we think we do, we often change it a couple times. There are some students who've known what they've wanted to do seemingly since birth. If you're the latter type of student, awesome. Use your job portal to search for specific listings in your area of study. Not only will this help pay for college, but you can likely get early "resume-worthy" experience for your career. Those types of jobs also have a way of building into even better opportunities when you've shown your passion and have built strong relationships with faculty and staff.

If you're like I was and unsure of which path you're going to take, then just look for a job that interests you. My first job at WCU was in our archaeology lab, simply because I liked watching Indiana Jones movies and wanted to see cool artifacts. For that semester, I worked my way through dozens of old cigar boxes packed full of pottery shards, musket balls, arrowheads, and hatchet-heads. I scrubbed them clean with a toothbrush and water, then categorized them into collections. It was honestly something I looked forward to each day and was able to plan my own hours since the lab was always open. It allowed me to destress from thinking about classes and enjoy the long history of each artifact.

Relaxed Jobs

The archaeology lab was an example of what I call a relaxed job. I had very little supervision and was trusted with my tasks in a low-stress environment. In relaxed jobs, you're typically seated at a desk and your manager will check-in on you sparingly to see how you're doing. You track your hours using timesheets, whether through Excel or on paper, and turn them in every one to two weeks depending on the pay-period. Clerical/administrative assistant jobs, like customer service from behind a desk or managing appointments and scheduling for departments, are the ones you'll most often see in this category. In fact, you'll find most of these positions on campus are filled by student workers. A benefit to this type of job is that you often have down-time while you're waiting for the next patron or task. You can use this to work on homework. Being at the job gets you into that "work-mode" where you want to get things done, which can be easily channeled into your assignments. It can be hard to get in that mood after you've gotten back to your room with the day mostly behind you. Use that down-time to be as productive as possible as you're essentially getting paid to do your homework. You'll probably be paid on the lower end because of the relaxed nature, but the downtime is a bonus.

Active Jobs

Another type you'll come across in your search is active jobs. These are essentially the opposite of the Relaxed Category and have you moving around a lot. You're likely to be on your feet most of the shift without much downtime. The most common examples you'll see are students working in the cafeteria and campus restaurants. Apart from waiting and cooking, there's a large variety of other active jobs depending on your interest. I've had several friends who are tour guides, Starbucks baristas, and maintenance workers like painters or landscapers. Just like in regular service jobs from high school, these can be tough and exhausting, but there's always availability because of that. You'll have plenty of work to do and extra cash to make if you're up for that type of labor.

An active job you may not think about would be driving student transits, which are small buses. You may not have these depending on the size of your campus as most private colleges are small. They're more common if your campus is larger and sprawled out, but can be surprisingly well-paying jobs. At WCU, food staff were paid around $8 per hour, but a student CatTran driver (we're all about our catamount mascot) was paid a little over $12 an hour! That's a nice chunk of change for a few hours of work between classes.

Hybrid Jobs

Like the name suggests, hybrid jobs are a combination between relaxed and active. Your tasks will look different every day, and that can be part of the enjoyment. One of the best hybrid jobs you can get is that of a resident assistant (RA). RAs are required to live on campus and manage a hallway in their dorm. For this, they receive either free or heavily reduced housing costs. On top of that, they get a decent paycheck, live in an individual room, and have good opportunities to network with faculty/staff and other professionals.

These jobs take a lot of commitment, though. You will have weekly times where you're on duty for a few hours, which could mean staying up until 2:00 am. Other regular duties include decorating your hall, hosting monthly parties and hall meetings, and follow-up interviews with students in your hall to check on them. That's the active side of the job. The relaxed side can be most of the time when you're on duty, especially at night. Rarely will many students need things, but you're there in case they do. It's very common for RAs to get a lot of homework done while waiting, so take advantage of that. Finally, you're also there in case there's a lot of drama with roommates. You have to listen to the students, talk them through it to some degree, and decide if further actions need to be taken. RAs have an important job and a lot of duties because of that, but they are also paid well because of that. As an RA, not only will you increase your income to pay for college and savings, you'll reduce your expenses more than most students can.

Another hybrid job would be working for your college's Information Technology (IT) Division. For example, WCU has several IT options for students, the main one being the Help Desk. This is a solely student run area where anyone can go for technical assistance. The student workers mainly play a waiting game with patrons as there can be shifts with little to no business or lines out the door. The busiest times are typically the first week of school and during exam weeks. My second college job was working for IT Services where daily tasks would range from repairing computers, installing new computers for faculty/staff, and collecting out of date hardware to store in our warehouse. My favorite thing about it was that everyday looked completely different, but I had to drive a creepy, windowless white van around campus to pick up the surplus. Not the most ideal ride.

Specialized Jobs and Internships

This is the last type of on-campus job I wanted to outline. Specialized jobs and internships are different from the others because they aren't typically available to freshmen. Often, they aren't even advertised on your job portal. These are jobs that, as the name suggests, have skill-specific descriptions. These are skills that you learn and hone through taking your major classes and build upon through these positions. On-campus specialized jobs can be assisting in research projects with your professors, developing specific programs, or working on various projects. My friend Sean applied for a junior data analyst role with WCU's Economics Department during his second year. While there, his job was to collect, analyze, and display various economic data for the state of North Carolina to where it was all accessible in a simple way to the public. It was the beginning of their North Carolina Data Dashboard project, but it was a role and skill set Sean gained interest and experience in by taking specific classes within his Computer Information Systems major. Internships are fairly synonymous, but they typically take place off campus and with other organizations. They can be either paid or unpaid. They're both jobs that you want to apply for in order to gain valuable resume experience. Even more importantly, they help you narrow your focus to where you want to work after graduation. To find out about these opportunities, whether as an internship or specialized campus job, you have to go the extra mile and meet with your professors. Tell them your interests and ask how you can get extra experience. Networking with them and forging a relationship is vital to this. It's how you get ahead and stand out amongst your peers, who may only be doing the minimum to graduate.

Side Hustling on and off Campus

When you've settled into college life after your first couple of years and have started learning your personal balance between work and classes, you can think about starting a few side hustles. Quite simply, this just means an extra job or work that earns you additional income on or off campus. It's a common thing to talk about among adults where typical examples include notaries, trading and selling cars, renting out house space, etc. But there are several you can do during college, too. It's important to note though that these are supplemental to your current job and not meant to take its place. Your job represents steady money and has a predictable schedule while the same can't be said for side hustles.

Some low hanging fruit of side hustles can be found in things you would normally be doing anyway but can get paid for them. My fiancé loved exercising on a weekly basis, so she decided to teach classes with our rec center. Two times a week, she taught a cycle and ab class, which acted as two of her weekly workouts. It was something she was going to do anyway, so she thought she may as well get paid for it. Another example is tutoring. Tutors are always needed as previous ones steadily graduate. Think about what subjects you enjoy and understand well. Maybe you can help others do the same. As you're teaching others the material, it also increases your understanding and better prepares you for class. It would probably be an additional six hours per week where you're essentially being paid to study with others.

Let's take some time now to brainstorm side hustles that aren't so obvious, but may be perfect for you. If you're an artist and like to make creative crafts, you can both advertise and sell your works online. The most common ways of doing this are either through social media sites like Facebook and Instagram or through Etsy, an e-commerce site for handcrafted and homemade items. One that could be even better, especially if your focus is more in painting, drawing, or graphical design, is Artrepeneur.com. This is essentially a LinkedIn page for artists where you can not only sell your artwork but also take commissions, network, apply for jobs, and post your portfolios.

What if we think a bit more outside the box? Maybe you could help local companies market themselves on social media. Growing up in a time where there's huge emphasis on the Internet and Social Media, college students are prime candidates to help a business with this. This can range from monitoring and posting to a business's social media feeds to helping them create ads and marketing videos. There's a lot of potential here as small business owners don't like messing with it and would rather proffer it off to someone else. That's where you come in and offer to do it for them. There's no harm in at least asking around. Make them an offer of around $500-$600 per month. Before you know it, you could have a very lucrative side hustle with just three or four clients! Web-based work like this is nice because you can do it from anywhere with your laptop and a decent internet connection.

The Student's Pocket Guide to Personal Finance

Those are just some good examples several friends and I have direct experience with, but they are definitely not all the side hustles to think about. Here's a list of several more for you to consider, starting from what I view as maybe the easiest ones both to do and get started in, to the most difficult:

*Note that a few of these are repeats from the jobs section as several can be worked as side hustles in addition to your main job.

- Babysitting or House sitting
- Delivery Options if you live in larger cities (Doordash, UberEats, GrubHub, Postmates, Amazon Delivery)
- Dog Walking
- User test websites at usertesting.com
- Tutoring
- Campus Tour Guides
- Buy and resell items on online platforms: Ebay or local yard sale sites
- Referee for intramural sports
- Lifeguarding
- Starting a YouTube Channel/Podcast
- Uber or Lyft driving for larger towns and cities
- Translator for multilingual students
- Design business logos
- Offer services on Upwork & Fiverr - Here you can create an online profile and resume around specific services you want to remotely offer people. Essentially, they're platforms that allow clients to hire you to complete certain jobs for and you build your profile around the services you want to provide. Then, you can either be contacted directly by a potential client, or you can search for posted job requests related to your interests and apply to them. These are very

useful sites to earn extra cash and gain valuable experience in job skills for your resume.

Summary

After you've lowered the cost of college as much as you can, increasing your income is your next step in paying it off. There are opportunities everywhere, whether it's with scholarships/grants, or working part-time jobs. When searching for jobs on and off campus, take your time and use this chapter as your guide. Find those that work with your schedule, allow you to save up, and that you have some interest in. Also, brainstorm about side hustles that may work well for you, specifically for your interests and your location. Lastly, work towards developing your relationships with your professors and learning about internship opportunities. They're huge for developing your professional skills and acquiring jobs in the future. Combining a steady part-time job with side hustles, applying for scholarships and grants, and using saving techniques from the last chapter will help you ensure you come out of college debt-free and ready for your next step.

Tools for the Journey

- ***Scholly.com and Scholarship.com:*** *Two great scholarship directories to use in your continued quest to pay your way.*
- ***Facebook Groups:*** *Use local yard sales and community groups for your college town. If you are interested in side hustling, you can use these groups to let the local community know you're looking for extra work and interact with potential clients.*
- ***Upwork.com and Fiverr.com:*** *Two websites to showcase your side-hustling skills if they're more on the digital side.*

Chapter 9: Should I Take Out Loans For College?

It's rare to discuss going to college without **loans** being brought up in the conversation. We seem to be at a point in our society where loans aren't just viewed as an option for paying for college but as a necessary part of it. If you pair that with the myth, "You need to go to college in order to get a good job," it can be a deadly combination. Not only can loans easily create a crippling financial situation for you, as they've done for many students, but they can quickly destroy the strong financial foundation and habits you've built up to this point. Since loans are so normalized, most students don't grasp their severity. In 2020, roughly 54% of all students had some form of student debt, with an average debt of $37,585 per student[1]. That's shocking, and it shows why we HAVE to take loans very seriously.

In my opinion, there are two keys to fully understanding college loans: the first is that loans should only be your last resort. In other words, you should only ever think about them after you've fully applied chapters 6-8 and still are financially in need and have no other options available. By lowering the cost of college and raising your income as much as you can, it's increasingly unlikely you'll need to take out loans. The second key is to learn how loans work and why students take them. By doing that, you'll see why they should be your last resort.

Types of Student Loans

You'll find that loans are the easiest financial aid awards to receive. If we wanted to, we could all go to college completely with loans, with some from the government and others from banks. With loans being this easy to get, it's tempting for a student to just take them. Working your way through college and applying for several scholarships takes much more work. It's also tempting for students to borrow more than they may need. When reviewing your financial aid award, the loans offered to you are there as well, a button click away from being accepted. This makes it seem like it's just more free money, and it can be attractive to just accept it all. This makes the problem of loans even worse. Loans aren't free money because they come with the huge downside of **interest.** We discussed interest already in Chapter 5 with credit cards which was an additional payment to a person or entity for borrowing their money. With loans, however, you HAVE to pay the interest. Credit cards were different because you could pay your bill before you're charged interest, so the more loans you take out, the more interest you'll have to pay.

Student loans are different from regular loans in a few ways. One such difference you'll notice, depending on the lender, is that your loan will most likely have **compounded interest**. This essentially means that you will be charged interest on your interest, where each additional interest payment will be higher than the last. That interest is added to your initial **principal**, which is the total amount that you borrowed, depending on its compounding rate. The rate can range from being daily all the way to annually. The more frequently

Should I Take Out Loans For College?

it's compounded on the loan, the more interest you're going to end up paying in the long run. One of the rough things about student loans is that they are usually compounded daily.

Let's break it down with an example:

Let's assume you borrow $10,000 at a flat or simple 6% annual interest rate. This means that you'll owe a minimum of $10,600 total if you pay it off in a year. If you don't, an additional $600 in interest will be charged to you each year. Over the typical four-year stay at college, you would owe a total of $12,400. The main thing to note about simple interest is that the additional $600 you're charged each year is always constant, never increasing.

Now, let's use those same numbers but with daily compounded interest. After graduation, you would owe a total of $12,712.24, an additional $312 compared to the simple interest rate. This may not seem like much more, but it does allow you to see how it can really add up if you have to get several additional loans every year at college. If you research different student loans or use the ones you are awarded, you can plug them into a compound interest calculator to see what you'd pay in interest overtime, too. Even though you aren't required to make loan payments while you're in college, the interest piles up every year and will continue to for as long as you have the loan. This means that, until your loans are completely paid off, you'll pay more and more interest.

With student loans, you don't have to start paying them off until after you've graduated from college. This **grace-period** can be different depending on who the lender is, with most being 6 months, like with federal student loans, while private student loans could be a little longer. The grace-period is designed to give students a little time to find a job and settle a bit before they're slammed with loan payments.

Grace-Periods: *While grace-periods sound like a good thing, they only delay the inevitable. You still need to pay them and interest continues to compound on your loans (except for subsidized sections) even during that period. You'll notice that regardless of the different delays and types of loans available to you, they're all bad because of compounding interest. It's the central reason we can so easily underestimate loans in the short-term but will eventually have a large long-term problem on our hands.*

In addition, student loans can also be deferred. **Deferment,** also called **forbearance,** is an agreement between the student and the lender to either further postpone the repayment of the loan or to reduce the overall amount that needs to be repaid. This is often sought by students as a solution if they aren't able to find a job after graduation or if they aren't able to make enough income to start making the loan payments.

Forbearance Rabbit Trail

As I mentioned in Chapter 7 and at the beginning of this one, students are bombarded with the idea that they NEED to go to college. It's a myth that says graduating from college is a requirement for financial well-being, happiness, and insurance against potential problems and suffering. That comes from a place of well-meaning but ultimately isn't true. As a result of that idea, loads of students attend college without any idea of what they want to do, and they're lost when thinking about a post-collegiate career. They often seek to latch onto one of the first degrees that sounds interesting, particularly those that are extremely broad and require serious focus to lead to a successful career. A few examples are business administration, history, psychology, and many liberal arts degrees.

This isn't to say that these majors aren't "real majors" or are wastes of time, but students often underestimate the commitment needed to turn them into careers. With these majors, you're studying an entire subject rather than

Should I Take Out Loans For College?

learning skills for a specific career. This means that students need to specialize and seek to gain internships and experience to have a firm idea of how they can use that degree. Furthermore, there aren't necessarily as many ripe opportunities in the job market for these broad majors as there are for more focused ones. Companies are much less likely to hire a job candidate with a broad degree that hasn't been applied in some way. Because companies often value a specialization in these majors, post-secondary degrees are often needed to gain the jobs that those students are looking for.

Students lacking the passion to attend college or who pursue these majors without clear vision often have a crisis on their hands post-graduation, especially if they have student debt. Leading up to and after graduation, these students have incredible difficulty finding a job in their fields of study. In fact, some don't even find a job in that realm but enter the service industry where a degree isn't the requirement. They didn't have the passion for coming to college, likely because they didn't or shouldn't have gone in the first place, and the chances are high that pattern continued into graduation.

To be clear, it's by no means unrealistic to assume it's hard for some students to find employment after college, especially if they are graduating in a very turbulent economy like my class did during the Coronavirus Pandemic. **Forbearance** is helpful to those students but is more often utilized by students who made two types of mistakes at the beginning: they took out loans when they shouldn't have, or they shouldn't have taken the idea of going to college as lightly as they did, both of which can lead to debt hanging over students for many years of their adult life. This is why I implore each high school student to deeply consider whether college is the right path for them and why students should primarily attend a public university over a private one.

Bankruptcy

Normally, when a person gets into a position where their debts have climbed so high and they have no hope of being able to pay them off, they have the option of filing bankruptcy. Bankruptcy erases your debts but at a very high cost of lawyer payments, fees, and the destruction of your credit score. In fact, your credit score won't be able to fully recover until after a seven year period. You won't be able to borrow much, if any, money, and if you can, it will be at an astronomical interest rate. While bankruptcy is the Hail Mary pass of starting fresh from debts, one type of debt that it won't abolish is student debt. Any loans you take out to go to college are permanent and will follow you for the rest of your life unless they're paid off.

Unsubsidized vs. Subsidized

So let's say that you've followed all the steps up to this point. You first settled on a major you're truly passionate about. You've reduced your potential costs as much and you can. You've gotten some scholarships, grants, and savings from working in high school. You've no other way of getting financial support, but you still can't afford your degree. Finally, the degree you're pursuing can be turned into a career allowing you to pay off your debt if you still have it after graduation. Some that are more costly could include medical, law, and engineering to name a few.This would be a time and the only time when you can start considering a loan. Let's look at the types of loans available to you, starting with the two types of government student loans.

Unsubsidized Loans are technically the worst of the two for undergraduate students as they're very similar to any standard loan, just with the added student differences I outlined above. The nice thing about unsubsidized loans is that you don't have to demonstrate financial need. They're available to every student, even graduate students, in varying amounts. Your college determines the amount that you're eligible for based on typical cost of attendance and on whatever other financial aid you've received. The

Should I Take Out Loans For College?

downside, similar to a regular loan, is that you're responsible for paying the interest as soon as you borrow the money. The interest can vary depending on the year or the semester you take out the loan, but it still has to be paid for that period. You can choose to delay paying the interest until after your grace-period has ended and through any deferment period who may receive, but the interest will still continue to compound and will then be added or **capitalized** to the principal amount of your loan.

Subsidized Loans are the other type. Like with grants and need-based scholarships, subsidized loans are only available to undergraduate students who can demonstrate that they have financial need. Your college also determines the amount that you're allowed to borrow through this type. With subsidized loans, however, the government (the U.S Department of Education, to be specific) pays all of your interest until after your grace-period has ended. It will also pay your interest through a deferment period. While no loans are particularly desirable, these are the better options for students as you won't have to worry about potentially thousands of dollars in interest building up. Keep in mind, it's likely you can't pay your entire way by subsidized loans. More money in unsubsidized loans is typically awarded over subsidized loans. If you're just a few thousand short, though, a single subsidized loan could take care of the rest.

Private Loans

If you need more than what your subsidized loans cover or you weren't awarded any, private loans could be better than getting unsubsidized. Compare the interest and compounding rates of your unsubsidized award with your local lenders. Choose the loans that have the lowest possible interest rates and compound the least frequently. While researching, be sure to check if there's a grace-period available or if you're allowed to postpone payment until after graduation. Just remember with private loans, even though you've picked the lowest interest rate available, your interest will continue to compound while you're in college.

Paying Off Your Loans

Regardless of what types of loans you have, you need to start paying them while you're in college and working. Just like it's important for you to continue working to pay your way through college, it's even more important for paying off loans. Incorporate loan payments as a part of your budget, allocating a portion of each of your paychecks to steadily pay off loans. Keep that up until they're eventually paid off. Don't use your emergency funds for the payments, as you could likely need that money for something for something else. Make paying any loans off the priority of your budgeting. In other words, don't forego budgeting for food and other bills, but pay off your loans before you start investing (which is covered in the next two chapters) into your budget.

If you have taken out multiple loans, it's important to have a priority of which you pay off first. First, look at which loans are already accruing interest while you're in college. If you have any, pay them off first, and then work your way down to any subsidized loans you may have. If you have more than one unsubsidized loan, start with the one that has the highest interest rate, then continue with the next highest until you've paid them all.

How you pay back your loans depends on the type you received, whether federal loans or private loans. For federal loans, visit the website https://studentaid.gov/h/manage-loans and you can pay them off and develop a payment plan. The banks or credit unions that lend to you will often have a payment portal for you, and they likely offer assistance you can use to develop payment plans as well if you want it. Budgeting like we've gone over extensively can act as your payment plan. Again, use your EveryDollar app to factor in your loans, and you can determine a helpful payment plan while also comparing it to your income and other necessary expenses.

If you graduate and still have debt, your loans will come due with a monthly payment, and you NEED to make sure you always pay it. It's like a credit card bill at that point. Missing these payments will cause three problems: 1) You'll be penalized with different kinds of late fees, causing you to owe even more. 2) The interest will continue to capitalize onto the principle. 3) Finally, your credit score will start taking heavy hits. After several years of building your credit, you don't want to destroy your hard work, especially when the next steps of renting an apartment or buying your first house may be right around the corner (milestones where good credit will be extremely important). To avoid this potentially happening, work hard towards paying your loans while in college. The faster you pay them off, the more money you're going to save.

Deducting Loan Interest from Your Taxes- *Similar to how you have the option to deduct college expenses off of your taxes, you can also deduct loan interest payments. You can do this with up to $2,500 of interest payments, and it doesn't matter what type of loan it is[?]. That being said, you don't want your subsidized loans to accrue interest just so you can deduct additional expenses. Remember, deductions are there to help you if you HAVE to pay for something, not as a bonus.*

Summary

Now you have a beginner's grasp of loans and the serious implications of having them. Loans are only there to be a last resort for you, never your first choice. They can be brutal and have done severe damage to so many students before you, but that's why you have your *Pocket Guide*. We've gone over many ways to financially prepare for college and how to pay your way through. You have the tools to apply to your college experience and even pay off loans if you have to take them out. Having them isn't the end of the world, but you now know what to expect.

Tools for the Journey

- ***Studentloanhero.com and Lendingtree.com:*** *Can be helpful with loans for multiple reasons, the main one being that you can use them to search for the lowest interest rate student loans from banks. In addition, there's plenty of information about loans that's well explained on the student level. Like with anything, you need to do your research before making a life-changing decision, and loans are no exception.*

- ***Dave Ramsey Show:*** *While Ramsey is largely against taking on debt, he has very helpful advice on how to go about paying loans off in addition to what I've already said. If you come across this Pocket Guide while you're in college and have already taken out loans, start listening to him a little every day in addition to reading his work such as, Financial Peace University.*

- ***The Debt-Free Degree by Anthony ONeal:*** *ONeal provides an entire guide of resources on how to work your way through college and come out completely debt-free. Be sure to check it out for even more ways to lower your expenses and increase your income.*

Chapter 10: Defining Investments

Now, we're getting into the good stuff. By this point, you've got a decent handle on putting some money aside with each check, and you're starting to build a nice **nest egg** in your savings account. That's awesome! Next, we need to think about the different things you can do with that money so that it's working for you. When your money's working for you, it's making you more money without you having to worry about it too much. That's a broad overview of what an investment is. Investments are items you're parking your money into so that it will increase highly in value overtime.

What is an investment?

This may sound similar to the interest earned in savings and money market accounts that we talked about earlier, but it's a lot different. One key difference is that your money is completely "safe" in a savings/money market account(s) and is gradually earning you a small percentage of interest for letting the bank borrow it. In this case, "safe" means that whatever you've put into it, that base amount will never decrease. Investments are more risky: once you buy them, the value of that investment can decrease, increase, or relatively stay the same. A lot of times, the value can change by a huge amount. So why would you risk losing money? It's scary!!

Why Should I Invest?

The main reason you should invest is to ensure a financially stable future for you and your family. You do that by building wealth steadily over time, the key to which is investing. By investing, you build more wealth than you ever possibly could by just putting money in your savings. In fact, it would be extremely difficult to be all set for retirement by just saving and not investing, but I'll touch on that a little later in this chapter. It feels scary because we often think about money from a very short-term perspective. It's hard to wrap our heads around building wealth over a long period of time, like years or decades. If you begin this process while you're a student, you will have an incredible amount of time for your money to grow.

When Should I Start Investing?

How do you know you've saved up enough money and are ready to start investing? This comes back to your nest egg. A good rule of thumb for the amount of cash to keep in your nest egg is six to eight months of expenses. In other words, if you weren't able to work for some reason, your nest is capable of paying for everything you need for six to eight months until you can get back on your feet. This is a common rule you'll run across if you read other financial books or listen to Youtubers. While the number of recommended months of expenses saved changes depending on who you listen to, six to eight months is a good goal.

While the rule itself doesn't change, your financial situation can and often will. For example, you may move off campus, which adds rent, power and other bills to your monthly expenses. As you get older you'll also have insurance, a house, a family, and other things that will lead to your nest egg needing to be increased. Your priorities go like this: bills are paid, food is on the table, savings goal is achieved, and then you're ready to start investing.

Building Wealth vs. Getting Rich

Building wealth is a journey as a whole, while investing is the vehicle in which you travel. We shouldn't think of this as the same thing as getting rich. Building wealth evolves over your entire life and requires work; You gradually expand into several types of investments and continue to use the **Maximization Rule** (Increase income, lower expenses). When we think of getting rich, we often think of winning the lottery or scoring it big because of a "lucky break." Getting rich isn't something you can count on and can go completely broke pursuing that idea. Riches don't teach you how to handle your finances; building wealth slowly does. The habits are the most important thing to learn, not the money. Committing to a journey of building wealth allows you to have a firm grasp on your finances and keeps you from having to solely rely on luck because on this journey, you make your own luck.

Your investments require patience. As a general rule for students, we should view our investments as "untouchable" money. This means that we don't need the money we're putting in, and if the prices of those investments change, we won't panic and sell them. Similar to the plan for your savings we discussed earlier, you gradually set aside a portion of your income to invest. This is the general rule for long-term investing, and it works well because time is your best friend at this age. I'll go over more specifics of this when we dive into each type of investment and how to invest in them.

Retirement Means Financial Freedom

We know that "Building Wealth" is the name of the journey, but what exactly is the goal of it all? The final destination is retirement. When most of us think of retirement, we think of an old guy sitting on his porch with a cold drink, yelling at the neighborhood kids when they get on his lawn and at cars as they drive by too fast. We think of endlessly traveling the world or playing golf five days-a-week. We think it signifies a time when we shouldn't work ever again. But that's not the retirement we should be pursuing. Retirement is when you've achieved complete **financial freedom**.

The beginning of our adulthood is defined by the need to work. We have to work to provide for ourselves and our families. Financial freedom means you no longer have to work because your investments have grown to the point of providing for you. Now I'm not saying that we shouldn't work or be inactive when we retire, but financial freedom means you can freely choose what work you do without having to worry about your bills. You can paint, write the book you've always wanted to read, improve child nutrition in third-world countries, or build the most innovative orphanage. The world becomes your oyster. That's why we invest and why we should start as soon as we can.

Social Security and Retirement

If we viewed retirement as being the same as financial freedom, we'd be much more prepared for the latter half of our lives. Remember when I talked about Social Security benefits in the Taxes chapter? That's actually tied very closely with how most think of retirement. Social Security benefits are income paid to Americans who are old enough to officially retire, meaning 67 years old if they're born after 1960. This is known as the **Full-Retirement Age**. We don't need to dive too much into this, but know that these benefits are calculated by taking an average wage of your last 35 years of taxed income. From this, one would receive a certain amount of insurance benefits and yearly income.

Full Retirement Age - *You are allowed to claim Social Security benefits as young as 62 years old, but they will be reduced by up to 30%. At 67, you'll receive the full amount, and if you wait until then, you'll receive an additional 8% benefits for each year after 67 that you waited to claim Social Security benefits up to the age of 70.*

Defining Investments

The common view of retirement is that when it happens, things are just going to be fine. That income won't necessarily be an obstacle to worry about. The idea of not working is so attractive that most of us don't think past it. We may also think that "we'll just live on Social Security"; however, this can lead to some problems, problems that many of us are already familiar with. Most Americans don't realize that Social Security benefits are much smaller than they think they will be. We aren't paid the same salary we made leading up to retirement, but an AVERAGE of the past thirty-five years of jobs we paid social security taxes on our income. That can even take into account those crappy jobs some had to work in their late twenties trying to find the right career-path. The point is relying on Social Security in retirement will be an income reduction.

Some companies have retirement packages you can invest in such as 401ks or 403bs. These are what a lot of people simply refer to as their "retirement." Investing in these would give the individual additional income when they retire. A similar problem to saving and trusting in Social Security occurs, though. Most Americans don't invest nearly enough in these accounts nor understand the significance of investing for retirement. The result ends up looking very similar when they retire: they have a lot less to live on than they thought they would.

Now, if we combine this common view of retirement with how frivolous most Americans are with their money, things become very scary. Like I mentioned in Chapter 1, spending money, lots of money, is in our culture. You can't overstate how dominant the "spend it if you got it" mindset truly is. Because of this, we have a very small view on how much we should be saving, let alone investing. We spend our money on things we want, things that make our life easier or more fun. The common mindset is to live the fun and flashy lifestyle in the first half of our life while also thinking retirement is going to be great. What this leads to is "retirement" into a very distressing financial situation. When folks with this mindset retire, they don't have financial freedom, not even close. Too often do people retire into a situation where they can't afford to keep with the costly lifestyle and/or pay the extra bills they created for themselves. Because of this, they have to work when they're older, sometimes even jobs that are physically hard on them for a small wage, just so they can pay the bills. This can be made even harder as health issues assuredly come up. If they didn't save for retirement, then there's no nest egg to help with emergencies either.

This is why we have to have the financial freedom mindset and consistently use wealth building habits, starting as early as we can. You reduce the flashiness of your lifestyle while you're younger, saving and investing your money, learning to live on less, so that when you're in the second half of your life, you won't have this stress. Remember, this doesn't mean you're only eating rice and beans or staying locked in doors on the weekend. You're just balancing fun with self-control, so you can achieve financial freedom. Financial freedom doesn't mean being rich; it just means you're taken care of because of the strong financial habits you've used up to that point.

Saving vs. Investing

So, what if we just focused on saving as a strategy for retirement? Most Americans aren't good at saving, so how far could we get with just keeping the good habit of the 10-20% rule? Bearing this in mind, we can run a quick Google Search and see the amount people recommend we should save for retirement. In fact, several websites will give a recommended amount for every 10 years to know you're on track based on the average expenses and income of Americans. The most common recommendation I found was that you should have saved approximately $650,000 by the time you retire. On top of that, another $11,500-$23,000 should be set aside as an emergency fund[1]. As we proceed forward using $650,000 as our example, bear in mind that the average American, by the time they're 65-69, has only saved $206,819.35[2]. Sounds like

Defining Investments

a lot of money, right? It's well over half-a-million dollars. We have to question this amount, though. Would that actually be enough for us to be financially free and truly retired? To figure that out, let's assume we retire at age 65, and we keep to these recommendations: we have the $650,000 retirement fund, the emergency fund that we'll call $17,500, and we also begin drawing Social Security. For an easier calculation, we assume that we'll only live about another 20 years, until we're 85. If we divide our retirement by those 20 years, then we will have a yearly allowance of $32,500, equivalent to only earning about $15.63 an hour. This is likely a big cut for most people from their salary leading up to retirement. We have to add social security to that as well. For that, we'll use the estimated national average for annual Social Security Benefit from the Social Security Association, which is about $17,000, giving us a total of $49,500 to live on each year.

Honestly, this may not sound too bad. It's a little lower than the average starting salary of recent college graduates according to the National Association of Colleges and Employees but is usually viewed as a decent starting salary by us[3]. This may not exactly be realistic for the 10% rule just in a money market account. You have to assume you were able to fully raise that $650,000 for starters. Imagine that you began working when you were 18 and never stopped working until you retired at 65. That's 47 years of work, each of which you at least applied the basic 10-20% savings rule with each of your checks. To be able to hit the goal, you would have to save $13,829.78 each year without accounting for interest. If you were saving 10%, that means your income would have to be $138,297.80 per year starting when you're 18. You can't tell me that's normal. If you were even saving 20%, you would have to be making $69,148.90 a year since you started working at 18. It's possible to reach the $650,000 mark just by saving into a money market account, but it would make things unnecessarily hard on you. You'd have to heavily lower your expenses, likely to the point of living with someone for the majority of those years so you could just massively save.

There are two other things we need to account for as well: life and Inflation. It's hard to imagine a life where everything goes just right up until you're 65. You don't have any emergencies, you bought a pretty cheap house and paid it off, cheap vehicles, and had a high-paying job/income for ALL 47 of those years. In fact, that would never be the case. Chances are that if you begin in a job earning $69,000 or higher when you are 18, you're already in a position of some wealth and won't have much trouble following the basic principles. But that's not the norm. Even when you hit 65, you're at a much higher risk for complicated health problems than any other time in your life. You're getting older, and you have to remember that $650,000 + Social Security is all your money, and it has to last you until the end of your life. That's assuming you can save up to that amount and evenly divide it up into a salary without spending too much of it.

Inflation

Inflation is another huge consideration for our savings. According to *Dictionary.com*, inflation is "a general increase in prices and fall in the purchasing value of money." In other words, it's the rate at which prices are increasing and the value of your money is decreasing. You're gradually able to buy less of something for the same amount of money. For example, inflation has changed the average price of coffee from $0.44 for a cup in 1970 to $2.70 in 2020 and this example can be applied to almost all goods[4]. Bearing that in mind, this would also make our savings worth less. But by how much?

Purchasing Power - *When we see our money devalue as a result of inflation, this is what's called a loss in our purchasing power. If our purchasing power decreases, it means that the number of things our dollar can purchase has decreased.*

Defining Investments

The current inflation rate can be looked up at any point. In February 2020, the most recent rate was 2.5%. Let's assume it stays at this rate for the 47 years we're saving. If we manage to save our $650,000 under our mattress, we would effectively lose $16,250 in value thanks to inflation. Because inflation is working against you, wherever you place your money, it at least needs to produce more value/money for you than inflation is taking from you.

This is where investing comes in and makes your wealth building journey much easier. Investments give your money an opportunity to grow into a level large enough for your financial freedom. Check out this example where we just invest $100 each month into a retirement fund. For this example, we're imagining we began investing that $100 since we were 18 to age 67, when we can receive Social Security. For simplicity, we're going to assume our money is growing at a compounding rate of 10% each year, which is the average growth of the stock market over time[5]. If we just did that, only $100 each month and no more, we'd have approximately $1.5 million by the time we're 67. And that's very little investment effort. You can see just how powerful letting your investments grow over time truly is.

Summary

This shows you the beauty of **compounding interest** when it's on your side, rather than working against you from a loan**.** This is why you notice such a sharp increase in the wealth built over time with investing compared to just saving. Compounding interest is one of the biggest reasons you'll hear several professors and many professionals advocate for investing. You build a lot of wealth over time, much more than is possible from typical savings accounts, but it requires tremendous patience. Time is your best friend, and you should allow it to work for you. The journey to retirement takes more than a day, and you shouldn't deviate from the path too much for the flashy distractions. Finally, the more time you allow for your wealth to grow, the more financially free you'll be when you're an adult, especially when you reach the age when everyone else is retiring. Now, we'll head to the last chapter where I'm going to show you exactly how to invest and set yourself up for financial freedom.

Tools for the Journey

- ***Investopedia.com:*** *All the information you'd ever want on investments and examples that show the power of building wealth over time compared to trying to get rich quickly or simply building up a savings account.*

- ***The Intelligent Investor by Benjamin Graham:*** *This is one of the most popular investment books of all time. It's advanced, and you'll likely have to read some pages more than once, but it's a must read in my opinion if you have an increasing interest in investing.*

Chapter 11: How to Invest and What to Invest In?

You understand what investments are and how powerful they can be. Now, it's time you get the tools that allow you to start investing. There are several ways you can purchase your investments. The differences lie in the type of investment that we're talking about. We're going to dive into the 4 types of investments that I think are good for college students to consider: stocks, bonds, collectibles, and cryptocurrency. These aren't the only kinds of investments by any means, but I think they are the easiest ones for college students to use to begin building their wealth.

Before we do that, I want to remind you that the money you invest should be in addition to your savings. In other words, have your nest egg/emergency funds of about six to eight months established first and always keep it above that. Furthermore, keep that growing steadily to a new goal of $10,000, so you're continuously preparing for life after college. Even though you're young, healthy, and in college, surprise expenses can happen anytime; your car could need a variety of simple repairs from $50-$500 or you could have a medical emergency.

That's why your investments need to be completely separate to grow in value, so you don't feel like you have a need for that money. To do this, you can start with the 10 -20% Rule. This percentage will be different for every student depending on their necessary bills and income, but it doesn't matter, as long as you're investing money you don't NEED in the first place. In addition to this, only start investing after your college loans are paid off. If you have those, paying them off is priority number one. There are the four basic methods you can use when investing or even use a combination of them.

What are the Best Strategies for Investing?

Let me introduce you to the **fundamental principle of investing**: **buy low and sell high**. Ideally, you should purchase investments when they're at their cheapest point and sell them when they're the most expensive. That would be how you build the largest amount of wealth. In reality, it's very difficult to follow that principle exactly because we don't know exactly how prices will fluctuate; however, there are ways we can still effectively abide by it.

 **Markets -** *Now that we're diving into the thick of investing, I have to start using specific terminology, one of those being the word "market(s)." Fundamentally, a **market** refers to an area or a system where people buy and sell goods or services. We apply it the same way to investments. For whatever type of investment you're talking about, you can attach the word market to the end of it. Stock market for example refers to the entire system of people buying and selling stocks. Generally, when I use the word market in this chapter, think of the stock market to make it easier to visualize. Investment markets have a lot of similarities so we can talk about them grouped together often. But for simplicity, think about them in terms of the stock market unless I indicate another investment.*

How to Invest and What to Invest In?

- **Method 1 - Selling High:** One method that I mentioned in the last chapter was thinking mainly in the long term. Because you're young, you can come close to really **maximizing the "sell high"** portion of the principle if you seldom sell and hold your investments until you've hit your 60's. A supportive reason for this is that most investments like stocks and bonds perform incredibly well over decades of time, which really works in your favor. Despite how the market moves in the short-term, you HODL (Hold on for Dear Life) and resist the urge to sell. You can't go wrong with just holding your investments until you're older; it's just hard for people to do because as humans, we can get emotional about how prices change in the short-term.

- **Method 2 - Buying Low:** On the other side of the coin, you can focus heavily on the **"buy low"** portion. For this, you're mainly concerned with very heavy investments at points when the markets are very low like during recessions. Recent examples are when the housing market bubble burst in 2008, leading to a crash in world stock markets or the stock market crashes due to the Corona Virus. If this was your main strategy, these would be green lights to you for investing. Historically, the market has always recovered to being in better shape than it was before each crash, so there is some soundness to this idea.

- **Method 3 - DCA In:** The best strategy for abiding by the Fundamental Principle of investing is by **dollar-cost averaging** (DCA). With this strategy, you maximize both the **buying** and **selling** sides of the equation. In short, DCA means to gradually buy (DCA in) and sell (DCA out) at certain intervals. With my stocks and bond portfolios, I only DCA in. Specifically, I have a set amount ($50) automatically invested every Friday morning, regardless of current market conditions. I don't plan on selling anything in this portfolio and instead, HODLing it long-term. By DCAing this way, I circumvent the natural fear we often have; our emotions tell us to "wait a bit longer for the market to decrease"-- let it get to a cheaper price before I invest. While that's understandable, waiting on that "right moment" can lead to weeks or months of not investing. The market could also climb upwards leading to feelings of regret because you missed out. An important thing to remember is that time in the market always beats trying to time the market. In other words, you'll build more wealth by allowing your money more time to sit in an investment rather than trying to time things perfectly. DCAing removes the emotions from your investing and allows you to just focus on the long-term.

- **Method 4- DCA Out:** You can go one step beyond DCA In, by using this fourth method. DCAing out means that as an investment grows, you pick certain points where you sell a portion of it. This allows you to lock-in profits, while also continuing to be invested in something that's performing well. Using this type of DCA strategy ensures you maximize your profits and minimize your losses in a market with high volatility because you're both DCAing in and out and taking advantage of the swings in the market. This is a harder method to use, and I only recommend it when you have a few years of investing under your belt. It's more important for you to learn to remove the emotions from your habit of continuously investing. You have to stay the course and stay disciplined. While I recommend

How to Invest and What to Invest In?

DCA methods the most for students, any of these methods can work for the investments in this chapter.

Never Lose Money

A huge reason people don't invest is because they're scared of losing money. They see how prices fluctuate, especially during crashes, and they're petrified of that happening with their funds. To quote the #1 and #2 investing rules of Warren Buffet, arguably one of the smartest investors and wealthiest men on the planet, **"Rule No. 1, Never lose money. Rule No. 2, Never forget Rule No. 1."**[1] There are two important takeaways from his advice. **First**, if your investments have decreased in value, meaning they're lower than when you purchased them, then don't sell them! You haven't actually "lost" money until you sell your investments, so don't do it at a loss. Keep with the fundamental principle and sell them high, not low. **Second,** don't be frivolous with your money as you invest it. Be smart and do your research so that you can make an informed decision about your investment opportunity.

Granted, we all experience fear and unease when we invest. It's magnified in turbulent times, and that's why you see the stock market steadily crash; people give way to their fear and pull out their money. Smart buying and selling practices, like DCA, and always remembering the basic rules can help alleviate it. When prices fall low, don't panic. **Stay the course** and hold on to what you have. When everyone else is panicking, keep buying in, but don't dump all of your money into the market when things get cheap. That's not the time to be a hero and invest your life savings. If you stick to these basic investing principles at all times, despite the prices and no matter the amount of money you have, then you shouldn't have anything to worry about.

Staying the Course - *Never panic or make a quick investment decision based on your emotions. If markets are starting to take a downturn, or even if they crash, that's ok. Don't stop your DCA investing. When this happens, it's called a bear market. This is*

*good for you long-term because you're able to buy investments at a discount. History has shown us extensively that for every cold market, meaning when prices either stagnate or see a heavy decline, a hot market follows. In other words, the long-term growth will continue despite the panics. You have to **stay the course** here because we never know how far the prices will drop before they resurge. That's why we can't invest everything at a certain low point, thinking it's the bottom.*

*We also know the reverse of this is true. For every hot market, a cold one is coming. If prices continue to climb, you know that something will happen to cause a panic and some type of crash. Another name for this is a bull market. But you also never know how high prices could get, which is why you never sell everything you have. You can't hope to time the market perfectly and expect to achieve financial freedom. It's always better to **stay the course**, weathering whatever storm may come in the market.*

How do I know if I have a good investment?

I introduced the impact of inflation in the last chapter and how you want your money in a spot that increases in value at a higher percentage than inflation. The same is true of your investments as a bottom line. You never want to buy an investment that's performing worse than inflation. My rule of thumb is that I like the investment if it has a return of at least 4%+ annually. This gives a nice cushion between it and typical inflation (2.5%). As you'll see, that sets the bar pretty low, as the stock market has grown at an average of 10% per year for a very long time[2], but it is a good standard to have for yourself when choosing between investment opportunities.

Stocks

What is it?

Out of the 4 categories, this is the one you've most likely have heard at least a little bit about, either from the news or in a class. Stocks represent pieces of a company also called shares, so when you buy shares of stock, you are buying a percentage of ownership in that company. If you own a high enough percentage

How to Invest and What to Invest In?

of a company, which is different for all companies, you will have voting power on company decisions. The price you see when Googling the company is the cost of 1 share of stock, also called the share price. This can range drastically between companies, like from less than $10 for a share in Blue Apron to almost $500,000 for a Berkshire Hathaway share, for example. Only companies that are publicly traded have stock you can buy. Each company can simply be Googled to see if it's public.

In addition to the price, some stocks also pay out what are called **dividends**. Dividends are when a company pays out a percentage of cash to its stockholders. The amount paid is calculated by taking the percentage dividend yield, multiplying it by the share price, then multiplying by the number of shares that you own. As prices are changing constantly, so do dividend prices. This is something you would have to keep your eye on as prices move. Beware here, the higher the dividend, the higher the chance the company is going through a turbulent financial situation and is trying to attract buyers to raise money. You can either receive your dividends as cash payments or reinvest them in the companies paying them. You'll also notice that all public companies have **ticker symbols,** which uniquely identify the company (APPL = Apple for example). Using the ticker symbol is the most efficient way to look up companies when planning to buy their stock or when researching. This is because several companies may have similar names.

The price of stocks moves based on the demand of the buyers. As more people buy into the stock, the price will increase. As more people sell their stocks, the price will decrease in turn. Huge swings in the market prices come from massive buys and sells by people. People are very unpredictable, making prices unpredictable. You can reasonably assume WHEN people will panic, based on when worldwide or nationwide problems occur, but you can't predict HOW much they will panic.

Are stocks good investments?

The American Stock Market has been around since 1817 and has had very strong returns of 10% annually on average. Therefore, the market as a whole has grown extremely well over time and has always recovered from recessions, panics, and depressions. Notice though that these good numbers are dealing with annual growth. While they perform very well over time, stocks often don't show that type of growth on short-term bases, and there are chunks of time when the market is very low, showing little to no growth. While the stock market has annually grown 10% when viewed from the long term, that means there can still be years when it has sharp declines or crashes. This is why stocks are great investments for students, but on a long term basis. Because of your youth, you have plenty of time to let them grow; only thinking about selling when you've officially retired and are ready to cash them out. Remember our retirement example where we assumed you only invested $100 a month in a fund consisting of stocks and showed you have around $1.5 million by 67? If you just invested in stocks in the simple way I show across the next pages, financial freedom is easily your future.

 **The 3 Truths of the Stock Market -** *Even with some of the uncertainty of the stock market, there are three truths we can always remember when making our investment decisions: 1. There's no "best" stock to buy because no one knows the future. 2. Since no one knows the future, don't believe anyone if they claim they know how you can get rich quick in the stock market. If they truly knew, they definitely wouldn't be telling you, and they'd be the next richest person on Earth. 3. The stock market has continued to grow at an average rate of 10% per year. No one has ever gone wrong investing in a broad basket of stocks and holding onto them for retirement.*

How to Invest and What to Invest In?

Ok, cool! But how do I invest in stocks?

There are two platforms that are perfect for students to begin investing in stocks. Both of these can be downloaded onto your phone as an app, which you should definitely do, as well as accessed through your computer on their website.

Robinhood

Robinhood is the first app I got involved with. It became popular because they don't charge you a fee when you buy stocks, which used to be a very normal thing. In fact, several trading apps still charge you a fee every time you buy. It doesn't cost you anything to create an account, but before you do, ask your friends if they already have one. If they do, they can send you a referral link, and if you create an account through that link, both you and your friend will be given a free stock by the Robinhood team. These stocks range from smaller prices, like Ford, to large, like Apple, and you're allowed up to $500 in free stock each year. After you've made your account, you can then refer your other friends to get them their free stock and grow your shares. I've often gotten a skeptical response when telling my friends about this, but it's just like it says: a free stock. Two things to note about account creation: **1.** You'll be asked for your Social Security Number because it is an investment platform. This is normal and is required by federal law. In part, it's to make sure you aren't doing shady things and because you have to pay capital gains taxes on any stock you sell that increases in value. **2.** You don't have to link your bank account to get your free stock. You'll be asked to, but you can click skip instead. You're welcome to use my referral code to get you started: https://join.robinhood.com/danielh9428

Through Robinhood, you purchase individual stocks. Search any that are on the market, and you can see a lot of information about each company from price and dividends to its profits and earnings history. There will also be several links to news directly about that company's decisions and ventures.

This allows you to learn a good bit about any you're interested in and make an informed decision. To buy, you connect your primary checking to Robinhood then deposit funds. After that, search for the stock you're interested in, then click trade. You then buy as many shares as you want based on what you can afford. Here you'll also notice you can purchase portions or fractions of stocks. This is a unique function that allows you to invest in companies with highly expensive stocks like Berkshire Hathaway (over $400,000 per share) or expensive funds like the DOW Jones (over $34,000 per share). Fractional trading is one advantage Robinhood has over other platforms. For most traditional ways of buying stocks, you primarily have to purchase a whole share at a time, but. with apps like Robinhood, almost all stocks are accessible to you.

In my opinion, Robinhood is the best individual stock trading platform for the beginning investor. The interface is easy to use and to find your way around, and you aren't bombarded by loads of high-end financial information. As you learn more about investing, you can try the other apps I mention in the extra resources section.

Acorns

This is a wildly different app. On Acorns, you build an investment portfolio based on your investment plans. by answering a few questions, and it recommends an investment strategy on a range from conservative to aggressive. The more conservative the portfolio is, the more your money will be placed in less risky investments such as highly accredited bonds where your money is very safe. The more aggressive the portfolio is, the riskier the portfolio; you'll have greater amounts of stocks which are inherently more volatile than bonds. As you can probably guess by now, I highly recommend either aggressive or moderately aggressive to keep with our theme of youth and longtime horizons. You'll build much more wealth long term, but can and will see decreases when looking at the short term. When you select this type, the next step will be to deposit $5, which will then be matched by an additional $5

How to Invest and What to Invest In?

from Acorns or $5 for free. You can use my referral code to get you started: https://share.acorns.com/dkhartness7269

You'll start to really notice the difference between Acorns and Robinhood; your money will be dispersed over many investments. For example, in my aggressive portfolio, 20% is invested in large international company stocks, 40% in large company stocks, 10% in real estate stocks, and so forth. Each of those groupings, which I'll call baskets, are invested in specific Vanguard Funds, each of which are spread over dozens to hundreds of companies fitting the description of each fund. For every dollar I spend, it's split based on those percentages, no matter how much I spend. This is a great app because you can start investing at any amount, whether it's $5 or $500. In addition, you'll also receive dividend payments from each of these Vanguard funds every three months!

There's also a unique feature with Acorns called Round-Ups. Round-Ups connect to you checking out and tracking every purchase you make. For each purchase, it rounds up the amount you spent to the nearest dollar amount, and invests that difference. In other words, it invests an additional .99 cents or less with each purchase. This is a helpful tool if you have a hard time remembering to budget for your investments each week or month. You rarely notice the extra cents missing, and your investment portfolio steadily grows.

Another thing to note is that there's also a referral program with Acorns that has different rewards typically every month. You're rewarded when the friend you refer invests their first $5 like you did to start. Then you both receive $5 extra/free. The more friends you refer who begin their portfolios, the more free cash you'll get deposited into your investment account. The month I started my portfolio, Acorns gave a bonus of $40 if you successfully referred two friends, and $1,100 if you referred twelve!

The BEST strategy for you:

As most college students are new to the world of investments, stocks are what I recommend as your bread and butter. The first thing to do is to take advantage of the free stock and cash opportunities offered to you by Robinhood and Acorns. Create your account, poke around a bit just to get a feel for how things are set up, and talk about the referrals with your friends. Doing this was a huge help in building my portfolios early, especially with the referral bonus of $1,100 offered by Acorns. As you're telling your friends about this, don't come off like you're trying to sell them something; just tell them about a cool opportunity that's available and show them how it's worked for you. This also allows you to learn more about investments and personal finances with your friends. You can support each other through your wealth building journey.

After you've done this, invest the most of your investment budget into Acorns. The reason for this is that it takes care of diversifying your portfolio massively, without you having to do much work. Specifically, you should create a **Roth Individual Retirement Account (IRA)** with Acorns through their "Later" feature. Set it to either moderately aggressive or aggressive. Remember, because you have so many years before you hit retirement age, you have plenty of time to let your stocks grow. By creating a Roth IRA, not only are you getting the huge benefit of having your stocks spread across some of the best performing funds, but it also grows free of capital gains tax. That means that regardless of how much that fund has grown by the time you're 59 ½ years old, you can access that money without having to pay any taxes on what you've gained. It grows tax free. This makes the Roth IRA one of the strongest investment vehicles you have at your disposal! The catch to this is that you can only put up to $6,000 per year into an IRA.

IRAs - *There are other types of IRAs than a Roth, but I'll just explain the difference between the traditional and Roth. While*

How to Invest and What to Invest In?

a Roth IRA grows tax free, a traditional IRA does not. The reason is, before you have income taxes taken out of your paycheck, you're allowed to invest into a traditional IRA. For a Roth, you have to wait to invest in it until after you've paid taxes on your income.

All IRAs have a few things in common, the most important being that you can't withdraw money from them until you're 59 ½ years old. While you can technically withdraw money from your IRA before you're 59 ½, not only will you have to pay state and federal taxes on that money, but you'll also have to pay significant penalties. Avoid doing that. You'll destroy the wealth that you carefully built, setting you back immensely from achieving financial freedom more quickly. It could take you years to build back what you lose from penalties and fees.

No matter your knowledge of investing or how interested you are in other investments, you should create a Roth IRA and then aim to max out that contribution of $6,000 every year. I recommend not even investing in other assets until you have enough income per year for you to comfortably max out your IRA because very few other investments will outperform your Roth, and the tax-free growth is an incredible financial advantage to you. Maxing out a Roth should be the baseline for everyone; if you're someone who gets overwhelmed by the idea of investing, then continue investing into your regular Acorns "Invest" account after you've maxed out your IRA. It's hard to go wrong investing in a wide basket of stocks and letting them grow long-term. Continue to grow your IRA with the DCA strategy, starting just as small $5-$10 per week and steadily increasing those amounts as your income goes up with college jobs and side hustles or if the market takes a sharp downturn. You can set up a recurring investment through the Acorns app, where it automatically withdraws that amount per week, or you can manually do it. Either way, start that weekly habit of investing! Once you max it out, start checking out other investments. If you don't remember anything else from this investment chapter, remember to create and max out your Roth IRA.

What If I Max Out My Roth IRA Every Year? - *Now you get to see the real magic of compounding interest at work. Let's say instead of just $100 a month, you're hypothetically able to max out your IRA contribution every year, starting when you're 18 until you're 67 like our previous example. Instead of ~$1.5 million, you'd have over $6.3 million! In fact, you'd be a millionaire by the time you're 49 from your Roth alone. Who can argue with those numbers? Now, you have your goal*

Bonds

What is it?

Bonds are investments that act as a loan from you, the buyer, to the entity selling/issuing the bond. You get to act as the bank or the lender as you give out a loan to a government or a corporation/business who gives you an IOU. Just like a traditional loan, you can expect to make money, or interest, on the lent amount. There are a few differences from traditional loans, the biggest being that the entity sets the terms of the bond. You purchase a bond for a specific amount called the principal. It can range in price depending on several factors, but they're often priced at a **par**(typical) value of either $100 or $1,000. With your principal comes a coupon rate and a maturity date. The coupon rate, or interest rate, is the percentage you'll be paid on your principal amount every year, until your maturity date, the point in which your full loan is repaid to you. So, let's imagine you buy a bond for $1,000 and it has a 10% coupon rate which will mature in 10 years. This means you'll be paid $100 per year. Then after 10 years, you'll be paid back your principal of $1,000, meaning you doubled your initial investment. Sounds pretty attractive when put like that doesn't it?

There are a few other things that go into picking a bond, however. The typical interest rate you'll be dealing with over a good bond is usually 3-5%.

How to Invest and What to Invest In?

Similar to how really high dividends tend to be indicators of an extremely risky stock, high coupon rates can signal that as well.

Risk

Bonds are given a credit rating by either Standard & Poor's (S & P), Moody's Investors Service, or Fitch Ratings Inc, which are all independent rating agencies. These ratings are alphabetical and range from AAA, which is the rating of government and well-performing corporations, to CCC, which are given to corporate bonds where the company is very likely to either not pay them back or file for bankruptcy. The higher the grade of bond you buy, the less risk you take, but the less you make in interest. Bonds overall are much less risky than stocks. Part of the reason is you can buy AAA bonds, which are virtually riskless because our government has never defaulted or gone bankrupt. The credit rating agencies are often very accurate with their ratings, making bonds more predictable where stocks rarely are.

There is some volatility with bonds. The prices don't remain the same, and the coupon rates change as well. However, they change much less frequently and by smaller amounts than stocks. Stock prices and dividend payments can jump or fall by 20-30% where bonds typically move from 1-10% prices and interest. Stocks are also moving every second of the business day, where bonds aren't. The volatility that does occur with bonds happens largely in part to federal interest rates for government bonds and based on the performance of the individual corporation.

Another factor of the low risk nature of bonds is that you can buy some at fixed interest rates and fixed prices. This means that, despite the conditions of the overall economy or the individual business, your bond's value and your interest payments will not change; they're locked in. Lastly, if the company issuing the bond does default, bond holders, also called creditors, are paid out first from the company's holdings. On the other hand, stockholders are the last ones to get paid. This is why stocks are considered riskier, as the shareholder has the chance of not being paid anything and the bond holder has a very high chance to recoup their investment.

What else should I know about bonds?

Bonds are fairly simple. We've already covered the most essential parts of them. I do want to touch on the types and categories, but only briefly as you only need an initial understanding of them in order to begin investing. You're not expected to be an expert from Day One.

Categories

Short-term bonds only take about one to three years to mature. You get your quick interest and then your money is repaid. Medium-term usually have 10 years before they've fully matured. Long-term bonds mature over very long periods of time, - generally 30-40 years. A common example I've seen of this would be an infant's grandparents buying them long-term bonds as a gift for when they become an adult or finish college.

Government Bonds are issued by the United States Government, specifically the U.S Treasury. As I said, these are typically viewed as "riskless" investments; there's little to no doubt your money will be repaid in full with the promised interest.

Corporate Bonds are issued by businesses. Companies as well as the government issue bonds in order to raise capital for various things such as maintaining their current operations, refinancing debt, or for starting new projects. Corporations like to take on debt through bonds rather than through banks because they have a lot more flexibility with them. After looking at the demand of the market, they essentially name the price and payout much lower interest than they would to a bank.

Municipal Bonds are issued by state and local governments. Think of your local town or county wanting to raise money to build or maintain infrastructure for their local schools. One way to do that would be to issue bonds. These are typically above the par cost.

Agency Bonds are issued by government run or government backed organizations like Freddie Mae and Fannie Mac. Unlike government bonds, these carry a little higher risk, depending on the organization. A benefit to agency bonds is that most of them are exempt from state and local taxes.

How do I invest in bonds?

There are several different ways to invest in bonds. The first is by going through a bond broker. You can find these by doing a bit of googling for brokers specializing in trading bonds or by going through an investment broker like eTrade. They allow you to buy several types of investments from stocks and bonds to cryptocurrency and gold. Going through a broker allows you to have the most power because you choose exactly which bonds to buy, and you know all of the relevant information for those bonds. Many brokerages have very high minimum deposits though, which are often $5,000. On top of that, there are a tremendous amount of fees you have to be careful of, such as commissions, trade fees, and portfolio management fees. eTrade is a common example of this type of investment platform.

You can also directly buy bonds from the U.S Treasury by going to treasurydirect.gov. While you're there, you can view all available bonds with their interest rates and maturity rates up front. There are no extra fees or commissions to worry about. You'll need your typical information like your SSN, address, and a U.S bank account. This is to only purchase government bonds, however, not corporate or municipal. When a bond is purchased here, you'll be given an electronic IOU/bond contract, representing your bond as redeemable at the end of the maturity period. You can also buy government bonds through a brokerage, but you'll be hit by the same fees as corporate bonds. Previous to 2012, you could also buy bonds in person through your bank or credit union. You would be presented with a paper bond contract which you would be redeemed at the maturity date. Those paper bonds can still be redeemed. As I mentioned earlier, it used to be a pretty common practice to buy medium or long-term paper bonds for grandchildren as gifts.

Lastly, you can buy bonds through large funds like mutual funds or exchange-traded funds (ETFs). For example, the less aggressive you are in your Acorns portfolio, the more bond funds you'll be invested in. There are some funds focused solely on bonds, which will spread your money over many different types of bonds. These are helpful because you don't have to do a ton of research, and you begin very diversified. It's important to understand, though, that you lose most of your power to choose with this. You're buying these bonds on the secondary market, from other investors, not the issuers. Finally, you won't know much about the bonds, such as when they mature and if they're types that can be bought back by the issuer prematurely. You'll know fairly little, just maybe what category they are. Folks who want to hold bonds until their maturity should buy them using other means, but if you aren't interested in researching bonds and you just want to incorporate them into your diversified portfolio, this method can be good for you. Acorns is our go-to app again for this.

Recommended Strategy for You

Right off, it's nice that bonds have much lower risk and represent a way we can earn some dependable interest. But, you don't want to fully commit all of your investments solely in bonds. There's the fact that we shouldn't put all of our eggs in one basket, yes, but we want to embrace riskier things like stocks in our portfolio, again, because there's a lot of time for them to grow in our retirement. Conveniently, we can again use Acorns to dip our toes in the bond market with both our Roth IRA and Acorns Invest accounts. A fully aggressive portfolio doesn't invest your money in any bonds, but a moderately aggressive one does. To be precise, 20% of your portfolio will be split between government and corporate bonds. The rest will consist of stock and real estate funds that disperse your money over hundreds of different companies, just like in the aggressive portfolio.

Whichever portfolio you decide to make is up to you. I recommend both of them for whichever suits your interest the most. I look at it like this: moderately aggressive gives you even more diversity, alleviating more risk, and it gives you experience with more types of investments. Purely aggressive allows you to have higher growth in the long-term, as it's fully dedicated to stocks, but well diversified in them, still alleviating a lot of risk. The bottom line is to buy bonds through Acorns starting out, because there are no fees and you can create a portfolio with just $5. It's easy to lose a tremendous amount of money through fees without even knowing it, and Acorns keeps you from worrying about that. There are also less details to keep up with, which can overwhelm investors trying to make the smartest decisions. As you increase your income with a career after college, buy a house, and settle down, then you can consider the investments that demand more capital upfront. You'll have it by then as you continue to be wise with your money. We have to realize that we can't buy everything we want to right now, but there's a lot that we can do with what we have.

Collectibles

What exactly are collectibles?

This may sound like a strange type of investment. Collectibles are rarely talked about compared to stocks, bonds and cryptocurrency. There's no news coverage about them, constant graphs measuring their markets, and we usually only think about antique cars or maybe high-priced art. You may even remember kids talking about baseball cards and trading them on the playground. Heck, maybe you were even one of them like me. When we think about collectibles, we don't think about them as investments. It's more like a hobby that's different for each person. The collectible market is surprisingly huge, and I'll analyze one that I'm a fan of to help you picture what I mean.

I've always loved playing card games since I was in grade school-- not Blackjack, but trading card games, specifically Pokemon and Magic The Gathering (I know, you made it this far in the book only for me to tell you I'm a big nerd). The value in these cards is incredible. Magic, the main game I both still play regularly and invest in, has several boxes of old cards worth hundreds of dollars, several in the thousands of dollars range, and the oldest series (released in August of 1993) that are worth **hundreds** of **thousands** of dollars! This means that not only is this a long-lasting card game enjoyed by millions, but there's a lot of investment potential within it. Something to think about: investing and collecting these types of items can have a lot of overlap. You have to have the intention of either gradually selling your collections or selling them at your retirement point. Just like any investment, they require time to grow in value and patience to keep.

How would I invest in collectibles?

Collectibles are uniquely tied to your interests. That's what you have to determine first. Everyone is different in this respect, but our overlapping similarity should be that, whatever we're collecting, we're dedicated to our fondness for it, its current value and what that value will grow into. Apart from trading card games as examples, there are also different types of currency like old or unique bills and coins, comics (especially gold and silver age), or various kinds of art. When trying to establish what this might be for you, ask and answer the question: "What niches am I interested and involved in?" When you've established that, then you can use the Internet to discover how its market works and what interest there is from other people or businesses. Trading card games can be easy ones to start with researching.

Like I said earlier, there aren't official markets for collectibles. They aren't regulated by the government apart from capital gains and sales tax and are only

How to Invest and What to Invest In?

talked about within those niche circles. Being niches, there are many dedicated people to that type of collectible. For Magic, there are millions of players across the world and there are constantly new cards and products created by the company, Wizards of the Coast. The products are then sold to wholesale distributors that then sell them to local game stores, both brick and mortar and online. This is the **primary market**. We as customers would purchase product from the game stores to then play with and form collections. What makes the cards true collectibles is the **secondary market**. Think of platforms like eBay, Amazon, or even Facebook groups. It's anywhere where we as individuals resell our products to other individuals. Folks collect them, creating a demand, and as the products continue to age, they increase in value. In the case of Magic, the cards increase very heavily in value. As the cards stop being printed, this also increases their value because now there's a limited supply. This is called **scarcity**. The sets and cards that were printed the least and are the oldest are the most valuable.

 **Scarcity** - *Scarcity is one of the biggest influencers of the price of collectors. Essentially, as you can imagine, the rarer a collectible comes, the more the fans of those collectibles will value it. This is exactly why almost all collectibles go up in value over time. You have to think, when a box of cards is printed, tons of people open them and continue to as the years go on. Some boxes get damaged being moved around shelves and warehouses. Maybe some are even lost. Regardless, those cards will only get rarer and more valuable.*

The secondary market is how you begin investing in your collectible of choice. Take your time and do your research. Learn which platforms are the best to buy from and the most reliable. Maybe you can form a deal with online/local game stores that want to liquidate stagnant products for a steep discount. Just like with all other investments, you want to apply the fundamental principle of **buy low and sell high**. The same techniques of

DCAing still work very well, the only difference being you'll have to adjust your amounts of cash. Collectibles are different from stocks because you have to buy the whole collectible at that time. You can't buy half a painting, or a quarter of a card and expect it to have value.

The way I apply these strategies to Magic is by looking at both the price people are selling the cards, but more importantly, what each item has already sold for. The sold listings on Ebay or auction sites are the true way of determining the **current market value (CMV)** of your collection and items you'd like to buy. The price of collectibles changes the least often compared to the other investments we've discussed, so checking on them monthly is what I've found to be a good practice.

Because we're college students with limited income, we can best purchase collectible items that are being sold below their current market value. For example, I only buy cards when I see someone selling them pretty cheap, or when I win a low bid on eBay. I never pay full price for them. This way, even though I'm investing in them for the long-term, I'm mitigating a good bit of the risk by ensuring I could make a profit if I wanted to turn around and sell them. When it comes to risk for collectibles, it lies in the resalability of our products in the future. "Will people want this if I buy it and sit on it for several years?" This can make them pretty scary as many trading card games that have tried to make it big have failed. In addition to my buying method, we can also choose a collectible investment that has several proven years of historical value and a lot of interest. Magic The Gathering launched in 1993 as the first trading card game and has only grown ever since[3]. This gives me a lot of confidence in it as an investment.

How to Invest and What to Invest In?

Determine the Rules

One other thing you need to do when determining the collectible you like is to figure out what the rules are. What I mean is, how does the product work, why is it interesting, and what are the nuances involved with it? To put this in perspective, with Magic, it's very risky to try and invest in single cards. This is because individual card prices fluctuate all the time, similar to stocks. Of course, you can make money, but it's easy to lose a lot of money like that. Instead, the real value rests in the sealed boxes or packs of cards called booster boxes and booster packs respectively. Each of these boxes represent a specific series of cards, of which a new one comes out every three months. So that's the first rule to understand: invest in sealed products, rather than loose products. You protect yourself against more risk that way.

Another rule: when the print runs for boxes/series are stopped, it signals the beginning of their value increasing. On top of that, the history of all existing sealed boxes shows that they all have increased in value over time after the end of the print cycle. This is the main reason I look at them as investments. There's guaranteed long-term growth, but you're never sure how much. When a new series is printed, the booster boxes all sell for $100, sometimes higher or lower depending on the quality of cards within. Some boxes, like the original Zendikar booster box (2009), are now being sold for around $1,000 on eBay. That's an average growth of $75 a year! That's clearly a strong investment, outperforming the stock market. But, a set like Dragon's Maze (2013) for example, had an impressive number of horrible cards in the set and was massively overprinted, so it's only increased in value to nearly $110 a box on eBay. 10% growth over seven years is horrible, especially when compared to stocks and bonds. Then if you think about inflation, you're just losing money. Not every box is a gem, and you have to be aware of that history and the opinions of the players before buying. These all represent the rules you'd need to understand before investing in collectibles.

Recommended Strategy for You

Collectibles are wildcards and clearly different from the other types of investments, especially since you're buying physical items. On top of needing the money to invest in a whole item at a time, you also need the space to store it. Both of which are very limited to students. It can be a lot of fun to form your collections over time, though, since you get to literally watch it grow and hold it in your hands.

Some of you may not even be interested in collecting beyond enjoying seeing the ones other people have. That's great, too. It's not a necessity by any means to invest in them. For folks who are interested, since there's no convenient portfolio building app available for this, I would recommend investing in collectibles very cautiously. They should be secondary to your Acorns Roth IRA, and something you build up very slowly. It's a niche market, so you have to take the time to learn it. Poke around on several marketplaces and look for deals. Join social media groups, interact, and ask questions. If you buy, use my example and buy products already discounted from the CMV. This way you could at least flip your purchases if needed. Flipping and reselling these items can also help you generate more money to use for investing. You can turn $100-$200 into $500 to then afford more collectibles or to help max out your IRA. I often say it's easy to invest, even with $5, but it's MUCH easier to invest in more things if you have more money available. Using collectibles as a means of generating extra money can definitely be effective, and it was how I was able to afford the few boxes I bought to start my collection. Once you have the bonus funds, then you have more freedom to enter these types of markets. Regardless, use caution, and continue to put the majority of your funds into maxing out your Roth. Continue researching your collectible of interest, then enter into the market slowly after you've maxed out your IRA for the year.

How to Invest and What to Invest In?

Cryptocurrency

What is it?

This is going to be the strangest investment we discuss. Perhaps you've heard of Bitcoin, a completely digital currency created in 2009 by the unknown person(s) Satoshi Nakamoto in order to revolutionize how we spend, exchange, and manipulate our money. When it was created, it was basically valueless, worth only fractions of a penny, but as buzz around the coin grew, so did it's price, all the way to nearly $20,000 per coin in December, 2017. It made people millionaires, even billionaires, who bought it very early. The excitement generated such a huge demand for not just Bitcoin but several other cryptocurrencies around the time. That demand is what led to incredible exponential growth in bitcoin's price.

People and companies are so interested in cryptocurrencies because of the freedom you have in using them. Almost all cryptocurrencies are what's called **decentralized**. This means that no entity or organization is in control of the supply of coins, which is limited, or regulating its uses. Furthermore, the **blockchain technology** powering each crypto allows for basic anonymity when you buy, sell, or trade with the coins. When a transaction takes place, both the buyer's and seller's information are referred under a public key. The public key is a long string of letters and numbers, which refers to each individual completing transactions on the blockchain. While your public key and the transaction data are all public, it would be very difficult to trace any of it back to you or the other individual.

In addition to this, the design of the blockchain also has heavy security. There's never been a successful incident of hacking or other malicious activity involved directly with the blockchain. I'll explain. When Satoshi Nakamoto created Bitcoin and blockchain technology, the blockchain was designed so that each transaction is recorded linearly and chronologically, making it "look" and function very much like a chain with blocks that are linked together with cryptographic hashes. Every time a certain number of transactions are performed with the currency, the blockchain gets longer, adding another block to that chain. Because of the linear and chronological design, each block stores the hash of the previous block connecting to it as the link in the chain. On top of that, each user is allowed to join their computer to the network, at which point they are given a downloadable copy of the entire blockchain. This means that there are thousands of identical copies of the Bitcoin blockchain distributed throughout the entire world. For a hacker to successfully disturb or harm a blockchain, they would somehow have to be able to alter 51% of the copies of that blockchain, across thousands of computers, at the same time. Furthermore, to even be able to change it, the hacker would have to decrypt the latest hash added to the chain, and subsequently decrypt all the previous ones along the chain, eventually meaning all hashes, which is next to impossible. This keeps the amount of currency, our identity, and our transaction data extremely secure, so it can't be altered.

How does it work?

As I said, Bitcoin was meant to revolutionize how we think about and use money. When you have a decentralized currency, you can make purchases and exchange it much faster than with traditional money like dollars. It doesn't have to go through a bunch of regulations or be subject to high fees. So let's say I have a buddy, Soichiro, who lives in Tokyo, Japan. He gives me a call and says he's been hit hard financially and needs some help paying for car repairs and other family bills. To send money to him, I'd have to typically pay several fees to wire it, as well as have it converted to yen. If I wanted to send Soichiro $500, it would cost several hundred extra due to those fees. On top of that, he would have to wait several days before he receives it.

Cryptocurrency provides an alternative to that. If we both have cryptocurrency wallets, I can send him $500 worth of Bitcoin in a matter of minutes. Other coins like Litecoin and Stellar Lumens exist which are even quicker, making transactions only take a few seconds or fractions of a second. Each wallet has what's called a **public key,** which is very similar to an address. Soichiro provides his public key to me, so I can send him his currency from my wallet. I tell my wallet his address, and it will send my crypto to him. I don't have to pay any hefty conversion fees that would nearly double my expenses, just small ones like mining fees, which cost only a few dollars. With this near instant access to the funds I send via crypto, Soichiro can withdraw them in the form of yen from his bank or pay for his car repairs directly if the company accepts crypto.

Mining

Mining is a process where people, called miners, verify the transactions that have taken place on the blockchain, by donating computing power from their machines. This donation of computing power is what allows for lightning fast transactions. For doing this, miners are "paid" or rewarded a portion of the transaction in the form of the mining fee. The fee is small to us, but miners can be rewarded a decent bit if they verify many transactions. Essentially, the more computing power they use, the more they can mine, and the more money they can make.

This process is what's caused so many individuals and companies to want to use cryptocurrency and has given rise to several hundreds, if not thousands, of others. Any entity with skill can create their own version of a blockchain, i.e creating a new cryptocurrency, because the code behind the Bitcoin blockchain is open source, meaning it's open for anyone to use as a template. With the creation of multiple coins, companies have become creative with the new applications for blockchain. For example, lending money in the form of crypto would be much quicker, safer, and easier than having to constantly go through financial intermediaries such as banks, allowing individuals to be paid the interest.

How does crypto work as an investment?

Like all the other investments we've discussed, most cryptos have a limited supply and huge demand is created for using them for all the reasons I just mentioned. Each is literally it's own currency, and most are separate from normal forms of money. They each have their own value and worth because of this. This is further influenced by them being bought and sold on cryptocurrency exchanges, two of the most popular being Coinbase and Binance. The constant buying and selling of cryptos, as with other investments, causes their prices to fluctuate. If more are being bought instead of sold, the price will increase and vice versa.

A huge difference with crypto though, is that it's extremely volatile. More volatile than any other investment. Stocks can move a lot in price over a several day, week or yearly period, but cryptos can rise and fall by 50-100% in a matter of hours or even minutes. That's how early investors of Bitcoin became millionaires in a matter of just a few years. Using Tezos, another crypto, as an example, it more than tripled in value in a few months ($1.20-$3.95), then plummeted even lower than when I bought it (at $.90) in just a few weeks following that. Some may disagree with me, but I would classify this as not only the riskiest investment in this book but out of most investments. Despite this, the growing interest from banks, individuals, and corporations show a lot of signs that cryptocurrency is going to be a huge part of the future.

Recommended Strategies for Crypto

Even though this is the riskiest investment we've discussed, we still don't have to be scared of it, especially if we just follow the basic rules we've gone over. Like with stocks, there are several platforms you can download in the form of apps or access through your computer to begin buying crypto. The most popular of these, and the one I definitely recommend beginning with, is Coinbase. Both the app and website are very user friendly, give you a lot of valuable information about the platform's tradable coins, and are fairly simple

How to Invest and What to Invest In?

to use. The creation and set-up of your account will take a bit of time for verification. You provide most of your information, including your SSN and a picture of a valid driver's license. Furthermore, like you would eventually have to do with apps like Robinhood and Acorns, you'll need to link either a debit card or your bank account. Again, the asking of your personal information is very standard when it comes to the investment world as your identity needs to be both confirmed and protected. They don't want anyone doing shady stuff.

After the few days needed for verification, you're ready to begin trading. This will be as simple as clicking on the coin you're interested in and have researched, then deciding on how much of it you'd like to buy. One thing to note is that you have to buy separate coins at a time. Currently, no index or mutual funds exist for baskets of cryptocurrency that are easily accessible like with Acorns. You'll essentially be making your own portfolio a few coins at a time. Once you purchase your coins, they'll be available to view in your portfolio tab where a line graph tracks the changing value of your coins over time.

Crypto investments should also be considered an investment second to the Roth IRA you're building on Acorns. Don't forgo your contributions to Acorns to put them into cryptocurrency. It can feel like a very attractive idea, especially when you see the huge and constant price swings of cryptocurrency, but remember, we don't want to view investing as getting rich quick. Don't try to be a hero and go all-in with your money. With Coinbase, you have access to the most popular coins so you don't have to worry about them disappearing or being scam coins. That makes them all decent purchases and more up to your individual taste. I'd recommend starting with the cheaper coins, ones like XRP, Stellar, and Tezos, that are all either around the price of a few bucks or below $1. $20 worth of these coins buys you many coins, where it would only buy you a microscopic fraction of Bitcoin. To me, this means that you have a bit more "confirmed" growth potential with them versus Bitcoin. Confirmed in this case means that the cheaper coins have a higher percentage to grow than

Bitcoin might. For example, Stellar Lumens are worth about $.04 each at the time of writing compared to Bitcoin's nearly $7,000 per coin. If Lumens increased to just $.50 each in the next bull market, that would be a growth of 12.5 times! In comparison, Bitcoin would have to rise to $87,500 for your investment to increase by the same percentage. While both cases are possible, it seems more likely with Lumens because their historical high was $.94, but Bitcoin's was about $20,000. As to which you decide to buy, know this is just my opinion, and you should buy the coins you can be passionate about, just responsibly, diversely, and cautiously.

For whatever additional cash you use for crypto, use the second DCA Methods. Steadily buy into your coins on weekly or daily intervals, maybe at like $4-$5 a day or $20 each week. This is because, again, the markets can and will move rapidly, and you'll probably get constant butterflies in your stomach. With those interval payments, you won't have to worry about whether or not you should buy-in or wait for a cheaper price.

Set yourself alerts on Coinbase and a mental stopping point where you either decrease your contribution to each coin or stop altogether based on the price. For me with small coins below $1, I slow down or stop if they shoot up by 3-4 times what I was buying originally, and for slightly bigger coins like Tezos, I slow down if they double in price from what I originally bought-in. If each coin continues to increase past these alert points, you also need to determine a DCA sell-point. Here, you either sell at time-based intervals, similar to how you were buying, or you sell a dollar amount of that coin as it increases in price, like for every $.50 it increases you sell $30 worth. This guarantees you some earned profit from your investment, but also leaves it room to spike further because you aren't completely selling out.

Lastly, when you profitably sell a certain amount of one coin that's performing well, consider doing two things. The first is instead of cashing the $30 out, convert that amount into a **stablecoin**, which is a coin closely tied to the value of the U.S dollar such as DAI or U.S Dollar Coin (USDC) on

How to Invest and What to Invest In?

Coinbase. Because they're tied to the dollar, it barely fluctuates in price, giving you determined value with that coin and ensuring that you keep the profit you earned from your well-performing coin. The second is to reinvest those profits. When you convert them into a stablecoin, look at other coins that are low and buy them with your profits. This will help you steadily grow your portfolio and take advantage of its movements. Using this technique, you'll be much safer while investing in crypto and gradually increase the size of your investment overtime.

Final Thoughts

- Use this and the previous chapter as you're staging ground for getting started. You'll learn what it's like to own an investment, watch its value change overtime, and get used to separating yourself emotionally from that money. Using the simpler apps and referring your friends will give you great opportunities to talk about finances with them and begin a portfolio. Chances are you'll form a small group that's interested in learning more, and that will fuel your fire to continue researching.

- When you're in turbulent times, people are freaking out, and market prices fall, remember to **stay the course!** Picture me yelling that to you each time you feel the urge to sell out. Ignore the hysteria and keep doing what you're doing. You'll be the one smiling while everyone else is buying toilet paper for their retirement plan and the one left standing when the dust settles. **Stay the course!**

- Continue growing in your knowledge. This chapter has taught you the basics and anyone can begin investing successfully by knowing them, but, as you get interested in other investments and want to diversify your portfolio more freely, it's important you research and learn. Take advantage of the additional resources I listed to keep expanding your knowledge of the investments you like and personal finance.

- Finally, if investments aren't that interesting to you and you only want a key takeaway from these past two chapters, remember this: aim to max out your Roth IRA every year. After that, you can just continue investing in your basic Acorns invest account. You don't have to do anything fancy. You don't have to study and research or have an IQ of 300. By just focusing on simple investing every week and every month as a part of your budget, you'll be miles ahead on your journey to financial freedom than you would be with just money market and savings accounts.

Tools for the Journey

More Advanced Investment Apps

- ***M1 Finance and Webull:*** *If you get more interested in stocks, I recommend checking out both of these. M1 allows you to create your own custom stock portfolios called "Pies" that you can invest in. Webull allows you to dive very heavily into analytics and research. There's a surplus of information, and the app gets complicated as a result. This app would be the natural evolution after Robinhood especially when looking at different pieces of stock graphs. You can also invest in some cryptocurrencies with Webull. Both of these have referral codes dependent on both you and your friend investing $100 to be awarded. Here are mine if you wish to use them to get started:* ***M1 Finance:*** *https://m1.finance/5uzi2J5hl-M6* ***Webull:*** *https://act.webull.com/free-stocks/us/my.html?hl=en*

- ***Blockfi and KuCoin:*** *If you get more interested in stocks, I'd recommend checking out both of these. Blockfi is a simple to understand app that allows you to both protect and loan out some of the most popular cryptocurrencies for high interest rates. This is a great place to store your crypto when HODLing bitcoin or ethereum or transferring a portion of your savings into the easily accessible USDC for high interest. Kucoin takes everything cryptocurrency to a new level. You can do almost everything on this platform and research complex graphical trends until your heart's content. Kucoin is a natural upgrade from Coinbase because it allows you to do very nice things such as high-interest staking, lending, and building trading bots. Ease your way into it, and you'll really like it.*

YouTube Channels

- ***Nate O'Brien:*** *A channel that I found really helpful understanding stocks. He's very accessible to beginners and friendly.*

- ***Dave Levine Dot Com:*** *This guy is all about cryptocurrency and has tons of content on it. He gives helpful analyses of current markets, new coins, and smart trading practices.*

The Student's Pocket Guide to Personal Finance

- ***Marko - Whiteboard Finance:*** *Investment-wise, Marko touches on about every subject you can think of. He does an excellent job of breaking things down, has short digestible videos, and is very open about how he invests. He also makes you laugh.*
- ***The Investor's Podcast Network:*** *These guys are great to listen to while you're busy working, walking, or cooking. There are not many topics they don't touch on and always have interesting takes. You'll be in good company with them.*

What's Next?

My fellow student, I've guided you through all of the basics of personal finance. Everything we've gone over are stepping stones to preparing for, not only college, but for your adulthood. We've laid the foundations for developing your strong financial habits through saving for the future and living on less. I've led you through finding your first job and managing your paycheck responsibly. We've peered into the depths of taxes. We've stood together at the fork of college and career. And you're about to traverse the rolling hills of paying your way through. Even more importantly, you've learned how to begin your journey to financial freedom through investing and the patience that it requires.

While on your journey, not only is it important for you to continue these strong habits, but it's vital you make personal finance part of your daily life. Talk about it with your friends, your family, and your mentors. Let them know what you're learning and what you're becoming interested in. While there may be some awkwardness or resistance to the subject, you'll likely be able to learn a lot. You can listen to the past experiences of those older than you and have their advice, and you can compare your experiences with your friends. Perhaps you can even inspire your friends and family to join you on this journey.

*Note to the Reader:

If you found this Pocket Guide helpful, be on the lookout for more in the future. This is only the beginning of the series to guide you through the journey to financial freedom. You can find me on Twitter @hartness_daniel for updates and other helpful financial content!

Notes

Chapter 1

[1] Internal Revenue Service. (2021, March 17). Standard Mileage Rates. Retrieved June 17, 2021, from https://www.irs.gov/tax-professionals/standard-mileage-rates

Chapter 2

[1]U.S. News Staff. (2021, June 4). Average Credit Card APR | US News. Retrieved June 17, 2021, from https://creditcards.usnews.com/articles/average-apr

[2]Hurd, E., & Konsko, L. (2020, July 27). Credit Cards Can Make You Spend More, but It's Not the Full Story. Retrieved June 17, 2021, from https://www.nerdwallet.com/article/credit-cards/credit-cards-make-you-spend-more

Chapter 3

[1]Ramsey, D. (n.d.). A quote by Dave Ramsey. Retrieved from https://www.goodreads.com/quotes/19772-if-you-will-live-like-no-one-else-later-you

Chapter 8

[1]Lippe-McGraw, J. (2020, May 26). How to Get a Federal Work-Study Award (and Borrow Less for College). Retrieved June 17, 2021, from https://studentloanhero.com/featured/work-study-programs-borrow-less-for-college/#:~:text=While there is no minimum,once you're at school.

Chapter 9

[1]Kurt, D. (2021, March 16). Student Loan Debt: 2020 Statistics and Outlook. Retrieved June 17, 2021, from https://www.investopedia.com/student-loan-debt-2019-statistics-and-outlook-4772007

[2]Federal Student Aid. An Office of the U.S. Dept. of Education. (n.d.). Did you know that the Internal Revenue Service (IRS) provides tax benefits for education? Retrieved June 17, 2021, from https://studentaid.gov/resources/tax-benefits

Chapter 10

[1]Downie, R. (2021, May 03). 5 Hard-to-Believe Retirement Facts. Retrieved June 17, 2021, from https://www.fool.com/retirement/2021/05/03/5-hard-to-believe-retirement-facts/

[2]Synchrony Staff. (2020, November 10). What's the Median Retirement Savings by Age?. Retrieved June 17, 2021 from https://www.synchronybank.com/blog/median-retirement-savings-by-age/

[3]Gray, K. (2021, January 22). Starting Salary Projections Positive for the Class of 2021. Retrieved June 17, 2021, from https://www.naceweb.org/job-market/compensation/starting-salary-projections-positive-for-the-class-of-2021/

[4]Karimi, S. (2019, July 24). The Price of Coffee the Year You Were Born. Retrieved June 17, 2021, from https://www.yahoo.com/lifestyle/price-coffee-were-born-090000198.html

[5]Santoli, M. (2017, June 19). The S&P 500 has already met its average return for a full year, but don't expect it to stay here. Retrieved June 17, 2021, from https://www.cnbc.com/2017/06/18/the-sp-500-has-already-met-its-average-return-for-a-full-year.html

Chapter 11

[1]Loiacono, S. (2021, May 19). Rules That Warren Buffett Lives By. Retrieved June 17, 2021, from https://www.investopedia.com/financial-edge/0210/rules-that-warren-buffett-lives-by.aspx

[2]Royal, J., & O'Shea, A. (2021, May 25). What Is the Average Stock Market Return? Retrieved June 17, 2021, from

https://www.nerdwallet.com/article/investing/average-stock-market-return

[3]Jahromi, N., & Michaud, J. (2018, August 28). The Twenty-Five-Year Journey of Magic: The Gathering. Retrieved June 17, 2021, from https://www.newyorker.com/culture/culture-desk/the-twenty-five-year-journey-of-magic-the-gathering

Index

Made in the USA
Columbia, SC
09 July 2021

41608885R00104